THE USOP HANDBOOK

A Guide to Designing Universal Share Ownership Plans For the United States and Great Britain

by Stuart M. Speiser

Published in Cooperation
with
THE CENTER FOR STUDY OF
EXPANDED CAPITAL OWNERSHIP

THE COUNCIL ON INTERNATIONAL
AND PUBLIC AFFAIRS

777 UNITED NATIONS PLAZA
NEW YORK, N.Y. 10017

ISBN 0-936876-46-8

Manufactured in the United States of America

For information on how to order additional copies of this book, write to:
   Council on International and Public Affairs
   777 United Nations Plaza
   New York, N.Y. 10017 USA

TABLE OF CONTENTS

1.

INTRODUCTION; THE TOPIC AND PURPOSE OF THE COMPETITION

This handbook is designed to assist those entering the 1986 essay competitions sponsored by the Council on International and Public Affairs in the United States and by the Wider Share Ownership Council in Great Britain, on the following topic:

> In 5,000 words or less, devise a plan for spreading ownership of [America's] [Britain's] productive assets broadly among the people, and reviving the economy, without confiscation or increased taxation.

Both of these essay competitions will commence early in 1986 and will close on December 31, 1986, with the prizes to be awarded in 1987. The prizes for the best three essays submitted in the American competition are, respectively, $5,000, $2,500, and $1,000. The prizes in the U.K. competition are £2,000, £1,000, and £500. Further information on the American contest can be obtained from the Council on International and Public Affairs, 777 United Nations Plaza, New York, N.Y. 10017, telephone (212) 972-9877, and on the British competition from Wider Share Ownership Council, Juxon House, 94 St. Paul's Churchyard, London EC4M 8EH, telephone (01) 248-9155.

After the competitions close, I plan to undertake publication of excerpts from the essays with an accompanying text that consolidates the lessons learned from this project. I believe that Anglo-American cooperation in the search for an ideal plan of universal capital ownership can be very fruitful, since leaders in both nations are searching for structural changes that will solve mutual economic problems. Your interest in this essay competition bespeaks some appreciation of those economic problems, and I shall not dwell on them at length. They are summarized briefly in Section 2.

As the sun moves from east to west, so does the metamorphosis of industrial capitalism. Adam Smith's ideas, the industrial revolution, and Keynesian theory came upon the British stage before moving to the United States. The same is true of endemic unemployment and disenchantment with capitalism. Some of the most respected leaders in Great Britain have turned toward universal or "citizen" share ownership as the next structural change needed to sustain the British economy. In the United States, political leaders still hope that welfare capitalism will restore the American dream, but it seems inevitable that disenchantment, like the sun, will move from east to west. Therefore, I hope that this doubletrack essay competition will tap some of the best minds on both sides of the Atlantic, so their conclusions can be combined in a final document that could make the Universal Share Ownership Plan (USOP) a 1987-88 political issue in both nations.

The wording of the topic has been chosen carefully. Spreading the ownership of productive assets broadly among the people brings into play the concept of *universal* capital ownership, and rules out such microeconomic plans as employee ownership. Nevertheless, employee ownership has opened the door to a more equitable economic system in both nations. Therefore, the relationship between employee share ownership plans and the broader universal plans that will deliver capital ownership outside of the employment relationship is an important part of this essay competition. Obviously, those who seek to democratize the ownership of capital would be well advised to build upon the solid foundation of employee ownership that has been laid in the United States and, more recently, in the United Kingdom.

By ruling out confiscation and increased taxation, the topic calls upon the essayists to produce a plan that will not redistribute wealth at the expense of its present holders, and that will not increase the tax burden on the productive people in our societies. The term "productive assets" is broad enough to include shares of companies, whether large or small; income-producing real estate; and all other items whose ownership carries with it the right to receive income.

Thus, the topic calls for a blueprint of a Universal Share Ownership Plan—universal in the sense of being open to all citizens; "share" in the sense of shares of company stock or shares in ownership rights to other property. This handbook is something like a smorgasbord, in that it puts before the essayists many of the ingredients that might be used in an ideal plan of universal capital ownership. The essayists are free to pick and choose among the various dishes and indeed are encouraged to invent their own concoctions. A bibliography section, following the Appendix, gives details of the publications mentioned in the text.

Don't be afraid to innovate. We are dealing here with a radical idea—radical in the sense that it goes to the very roots of the problems we seek to eradicate. We are trying to treat the diseases of our economic systems rather than the symptoms. But the kind of radical changes we seek would not change our societies except to make them more democratic, more capitalistic, and more equitable than they are now.

We hope to design a plan that will appeal to all segments of our societies and all of our major political parties. That is a big order, but, as you will see, the early spadework has shown that the concept of very broad capital ownership appeals to almost everyone, particularly if it can be accomplished without confiscation or increased taxation. Therefore, keep in mind that we are looking for a *consensus* plan, one that will be acceptable to political leaders across the board, because universal share ownership will require extensive legislative changes. In both nations, our politicians generally are reluctant to advocate structural changes lest they be branded radical, even though radical remedies may be needed to get to the roots of deep-seated problems. That leaves it up to us—the media and the public—to initiate real solutions to our fundamental problems.

Try to resist the temptation to dwell on the evils of capitalism. If USOP is to succeed, it must capture the imagination of British and American legislators who cling to capitalist principles. We need ideas that will make USOP attractive to business and financial leaders, rather than those that smack of a giveaway or require a level of redistribution that amounts to confiscation.

As we fix our sights on the roots of our economic problems, let us imagine that we are working together on a high-priority design program to progress from the biplane that the Wright brothers first flew at Kitty Hawk, North Carolina, in 1905, to a 21st-century version of the Concorde. This time, it will be an Anglo-American Concorde designed to carry a very big payload.

The Kitty Hawk model of USOP (described in Section 3) was assembled by me from pieces of other ideas and a few of my own innovations. It has flown a few feet experimentally, through laboratory testing by the Joint Economic Committee of the United States Congress, the Brookings Institution, and a symposium of the *Journal of Post-Keynesian Economics*. But now it needs to be redesigned to ride on the thrust generated by employee ownership, creating enough lift to carry the American and British economies into the next century.

While the essay competitions in the United States and Great Britain will be judged separately by different judges, this handbook is being distributed to entrants in both contests. I have done my best to treat the two economies separately where there are differences, but the reader must realize that I am much more familiar with the American economy than that of Great Britain. If I sometimes lapse into use of the American term *corporation*, British readers should understand this to mean a limited company, rather than a government-owned British corporation. *Stock* and *shares* are interchangeable, as are *stockholder* and *shareholder*. *Common stock* means ordinary shares, and *preferred stock* means preference shares. *Billion* means a thousand million, as in the European *milliard*, and *trillion* means a thousand billion. All dollars are U.S. dollars.

In the sections following that deal with specific elements of Universal Share Ownership Plans—the smorgasbord dishes—you will often find questions suggested for essay discussion, followed by one or more answers, usually formulated by me. Please do not feel bound by the answers I have given. You are free to disregard or even to contradict such answers, which were inserted merely to stimulate discussion and to apprise you of some of the Kitty Hawk-phase thinking on USOP.

As we embark on the adventure of a new idea, it seems appropriate to borrow the last two sentences from the preface written in 1936 by John Maynard Keynes for his classic, *The General Theory of Employment, Interest and Money*:

> The ideas which are here expressed so laboriously are extremely simple and should be obvious. The difficulty lies, not in the new ideas, but in escaping from the old ones, which ramify, for those brought up as most of us have been, into every corner of our minds.

I have now supplied you with at least three job descriptions: aircraft designer, smorgasbord chef, and escape artist from old ideas. Whichever image you choose, it is now time to get down to the hard facts and even harder choices.

2.

NEED FOR STRUCTURAL CHANGE; INDIVIDUAL OWNERSHIP OF THE MEANS OF PRODUCTION; EMPLOYEE OWNERSHIP DISTINGUISHED FROM UNIVERSAL OWNERSHIP

2a.   The Need for Structural Change

Economic theory has yet to develop any cure for the cycles of unemployment and stagflation that bedevil the economic systems of the United States and Great Britain. Both nations are also beset by the tension between capitalism and democracy. Economic expectations have a way of ripening into "entitlements" in democracies, where the balance of voting power is held by the huge majority of people who are noncapitalists. This gives rise to pressures which, in the opinion of eminent conservative economists such as Joseph Schumpeter and Frederick A. Hayek, are likely to create a welfare state so unmanageable that it will bring about the self-destruction of capitalism. Indeed, Schumpeter called the American mixed economy "capitalism in an oxygen tent." And Dr. Arthur F. Burns (the conservative economist who may be the last man in America to part his hair down the middle) said in speeches as far back as 1975, when he was chairman of the Board of Governors of the Federal Reserve System, that capitalism would not survive without structural changes.

Dr. Burns did not specify what those changes should be. Most of our economists are preoccupied with improving methods of providing employment and welfare, ignoring the possibility that broader ownership of productive capital could make income distribution more equitable and could bring us other economic and social benefits.

Unless you believe that capitalism has spiritual qualities, or that growth and increased welfare spending can sustain it *ad infinitum*, you probably perceive the need for structural change. Let us briefly examine the problems of the present system and the potential structural changes available.

Welfare capitalism is supposed to provide enough good jobs to distribute income equitably throughout the population, even though some people will be richer than others. When the system fails to do this, the government intervenes and tries to redistribute some income so that everyone can live decently. But mounting evidence throughout the world indicates that the welfare state based on transfer payments is inherently inflationary, and therefore unworkable.

Today, as we try to sustain economic growth, we face many stubborn problems: recurring inflation, huge budget deficits, high interest rates, capital shortages, and massive transfer payments for Social Security and welfare programs that cannot be cut from the budget under the present system. We don't have the money needed to maintain national security in the face of the escalating arms race. We are suffering an erosion of the work ethic because many people find it more profitable not to work. We are also threatened by insolvency of school systems, local and state governments, and the Social Security program. As a result of all these problems, millions of our people feel alienated—shut out of our economic system permanently—and this is one of the causes of our crime epidemic. Respect for law and private property is probably at the lowest level in our history, lower today than it was in the Wild West of the last century. And even in these days of so-called economic recovery in the late 1980s, the gap between the rich and the poor is widening.

And what is the political answer to all these problems, both in America and Britain? Most of our politicians are still trying to solve them solely through jobs and transfer payments, although leaders of the SDP-Liberal alliance in Great Britain have started to look at citizen capital ownership as a possible solution.

Senator Russell B. Long of Louisiana has been the leading American proponent of broadened capital ownership. In a May 1981 speech on the Senate floor, Senator Long said:

> The benefits of Government-stimulated economic growth have traditionally trickled down through higher wages, expansion in the number of jobs, and the availability of increased tax revenues to fund expanded social programs. That approach has produced strains on the economy as the benefits of this growth have resulted in the accumulation of massive amounts of productive capital by a relatively few households while the vast majority have been left with only a meager net worth. Attention must be given to new ways to distribute the benefits of this growth more widely. Despite all the fine populist oratory and good intentions of great men like Franklin Delano Roosevelt, Harry Truman, Dwight Eisenhower, John Kennedy, and Lyndon Johnson, the distribution of wealth among Americans, in relative terms, is about the same today as it was when Herbert Hoover succeeded Calvin Coolidge.

What Senator Long was pointing to was the failure of the so-called "trickledown" theory of economics, which holds that the profits reaped by the owning class will *trickle down* to the workers and other nonowners—in the form of jobs and increased federal revenues available for transfer payments—and spread throughout society. It sounds good in theory, and until recently, most Americans believed that it actually worked, creating jobs and sustaining the relatively high standard of living that many Americans had achieved. But as that standard of living slips and much of the world moves away from capitalism, the days of trickledown may be numbered. Its success depends largely upon its ability to create jobs, and that ability is rapidly declining.

One important reason for our decreased ability to create jobs is that economists and governments alike are attempting to solve economic problems through increased automation, computerization, and robotization. They hope that the rise in productivity will make the economy grow, and that high technology will spawn new industries and new jobs to replace the manufacturing jobs lost to Japan and to Third World nations where labor costs are lower. But we are learning that while increased savings and investment in automation do increase productivity and wealth, they do not necessarily increase employment or economic equity. While the United States, Great Britain, and all of the other OECD nations are seeking to promote the formation of many new small businesses through high technology, it would take thousands upon thousands of successful small businesses to make up for the loss of jobs caused by automation. And even within the smaller companies, the management is using machines rather than people, wherever possible.

One of the leading experts on this subject is Dr. James S. Albus, director of the Industrial Systems Division of the U.S. Bureau of Standards. Dr. Albus forecasts the coming of a new industrial revolution which will change the world every bit as profoundly as the first one. But in his 1981 book, *People's Capitalism: The Economics of the Robot Revolution*, he warned:

> Unfortunately, the present economic system is not structured to deal with the implications of a robot revolution. There presently exists no means by which average people can benefit from the unprecedented potentials of the next generation of industrial technology. Quite to the contrary, under the present economic system, the widespread deployment of automatic factories would threaten jobs and undermine the financial security of virtually every American family. [pp.ii-iii]

As the importance of capital increases in relation to labor, it is clear that if we are to make a meaningful structural change, it must be in the direction of broadened capital ownership. But under present economic theory, capitalism has no safety valve. As shown by the British and European experiences, the only known method of structural change in ownership of the means of production is to move from capitalism directly to socialism.

But there *is* a way to make a structural change in capital ownership which does not lead to socialism. Indeed, it leads away from the use of socialist remedies for failing capitalism—remedies upon which we have depended for the past half-century.

2b. Individual Ownership of the Means of Production

Americans and Britons obtain their financial support in four ways: by working for it (wages); by receiving government checks (welfare); by cheating (crime, tax evasion, welfare fraud, etc.); and by receiving the return on invested capital (capitalist income). The first three methods have been used throughout the world for centuries and have often been fostered by government policies. The fourth, return on invested capital, has never been used as a method of creating an equitable distribution of income. It has remained the sole province of the rich—the "capitalists" who have the savings to buy corporate shares and other forms of income-producing capital.

Wages are obviously the ideal method of supporting people, and as long as our traditional capitalism was able to create enough decent jobs for those who wanted them, it was acceptable to most of us. But in an increasingly automated era, it has become apparent that no government—regardless of political bent—can create enough jobs to support everyone through wages. The attempt to create equitable income distribution through jobs, while the machines and computers produced by industrialization actually destroy jobs, causes a basic contradiction in industrial societies. Indeed, welfare capitalism is a system at war with itself.

The first three methods of support—wages, welfare, and cheating—are used by virtually all economic systems. Only the fourth method is unique to capitalism, and thus far the politicians in capitalist nations have allowed capitalist income to be restricted to a very small pinnacle class, while they promise to train millions of people for nonexistent jobs. Thus, the importance of this essay competition, which seeks to fashion capitalist income (the only method of support that has not been tried and found wanting) into a new political tool to solve our economic and social problems.

Of course, the spread of socialism has caused some structural changes in the ownership of the means of production. I use socialism here in the sense of government ownership of the *means of production* (MOP). In Great Britain and in much of the world apart from the United States, socialist governments have had a crack at using state ownership to solve economic and social problems. But after more than a half a century of experience, and despite the fact that the concept of socialism has natural appeal to the great majority of voters in democratic nations who are noncapitalists, socialism simply has not been made to work. As John Kenneth Galbraith put it in his 1978 book, *Almost Everyone's Guide to Economics*:

> If economic performance in a socialist society had come as easily and with prospects as brilliant intellectually and otherwise as Marx took for granted (and Lenin also, before it became, for him, a matter of practical experience), there would be no capitalism left. No power or propaganda would have led people to capitalism. [p. 22]

Socialism seems hard put to match the drive and creative energy stirred by capitalism's appeal to self-interest. Socialism also has a tendency to concentrate both economic and political power in the hands of an elite few—the same tendency that threatens the survival of democratic institutions. As John Adams wrote in 1776, when America was yet to be industrialized and land was the principal form of capital:

> The only possible way, then, of preserving the balance of power on the side of equal liberty and public virtue, is to make the acquisition of land easy to every member of society...so that the multitude may be possessed of landed estates. If the multitude is possessed of the balance of real estate, the multitude will have the balance of power, and in that case the multitude will take care of the liberty, virtue and interest of the multitude in all acts of government.

The world is ready for the next economic system. Capitalism and socialism are converging, if only because the repeated failures of both have produced a natural flow toward accommodation. So, in our quest for a new and meaningful structural change, we must focus on ownership of productive capital. It is the only change that has not been tried—apart from the socialist experiment with state ownership, which is really the opposite of what we are seeking: a plan of universal *individual* capital ownership.

While many people look upon the United States as the land of widespread ownership, the few statistics available tell a different story. As Ronald Reagan said in February of 1975, when he was a privately employed radio commentator:

> Roughly 94 percent of the people in capitalist America make their living from wages or salaries. Only 6 percent are true capitalists in the sense of deriving their income from ownership of the means of production.

It is difficult to obtain exact statistics on how many Americans actually receive substantial income from MOP ownership, but certainly someone as conservative as Ronald Reagan should not wish to minimize the diffusion of ownership under our present system.

Dr. Robert Hamrin spent four years studying future economic growth as a staff economist for the Joint Economic Committee of Congress (JEC). In a 1976 staff study for the JEC based on the latest statistics then available, Hamrin found that half the individually owned corporate stock was owned by the richest 1.04 million Americans (one-half of 1 percent of the population). In his 1980 book, *Managing Growth in the 1980s: Toward a New Economics*, Hamrin analyzed the privately held wealth of the nation and concluded that only about 5 percent of

Americans really share in the benefits of capital ownership (pp. 261-2). In this respect, the great egalitarian economy of the United States is on about the same level as the economy of India.

In 1981, the New York Stock Exchange proudly reported that some 32 million Americans (14.4 percent of the population) were individual owners of corporate stock and mutual fund shares. But closer examination reveals that only one-sixth of these shareholders (5.9 million Americans) owned shares worth $25,000 or more; and only 3.1 million owned shares worth $50,000 or more. Given the present state of dividends, the average annual return on portfolios worth $25,000 to $50,000 would be less than $5,000. Therefore, no more than 3 to 5 million Americans receive more than $5,000 of their annual income from stock ownership. Of course, there are other important sources of capitalist income, such as income-producing real estate, savings accounts, and bonds—but the studies indicate that the same pinnacle class owns most of those assets as well.

It is interesting to note that this figure of 6 percent (or less) of the population controlling the means of production is duplicated in the Soviet Union where membership of the Communist Party (which controls the MOP) is just about 6 percent of the total population. Thus, at the very moment in history when capitalism and communism are engaged in a death struggle arising (at least partially) from their differing ownership ideologies, it is plain that neither system provides substantial socialization of the income derived from MOP ownership.

Note that we are talking here about individual ownership. Shares owned by pension funds and other institutional investors do not make their beneficiaries capitalists, since the beneficiaries do not own any shares individually and do not receive income from MOP ownership before retirement. Even then, they receive the fruits of labor rather than capital.

In Great Britain the number of shareholders actually declined from about 2.5 million in 1958 to about 1.75 million in 1979. Since 1979, the number of shareholders is said to have nearly doubled, but this would total no more than 3.5 million shareholders in a population of 56 million. I have not been able to find statistics on the number of British shareholders who receive substantial income (£3,500 or more) from stock ownership, but it seems clear that the total is well under a million, since less than 20 percent of British shareholders own as much as £10,000 worth of stock. At the American ratio of one-sixth of shareholders owning enough stock to qualify, the British total would be about 580,000 people, which is barely 1 percent of the population.

The need for structural change in individual capital ownership was demonstrated by Cambridge Professor James E. Meade more than twenty years ago in his landmark work, *Efficiency, Equality, and the Ownership of Property*, particularly in Chapter 5, "A Property-Owning Democracy." More recently, Professor Meade restated his thesis in Full Employment, New Technologies, and the Distribution of Income," in the *Journal of Social Policy*, Vol. 13, Part 2, April 1984:

> My thesis is a simple, straightforward one. I am of the opinion that in the sort of Mixed Society-Mixed Economy in which we live ... there is now need for a fundamental shift of attitudes and reform of institutions; much less emphasis must be put upon using prices, and in particular upon using the price of labour, as a major instrument for achieving a fair and acceptable distribution of income; much more emphasis must be put upon the setting of prices so as to obtain a full and efficient use of resources and in particular of labour; and much more attention must be paid to measures other than price and wage setting in order to achieve a fair and acceptable distribution of income and property. I believe that this necessary shift of emphasis demands far-reaching changes in economic institutions and in social and political ideas. [p.130]

Professor Meade's answer to the problem thus defined is "to attempt to devise wage-setting institutions which would allow the real wage to fall to the extent necessary to provide employment opportunities to all who sought them, but to combine this with fiscal and other institutions which ensured that directly or indirectly everyone enjoyed a fair share of the profits earned on the robots, computers and tapes, and indeed on property in general." (pp. 139-40)

Another early English advocate of the use of capital ownership to bring about equitable income distribution was Nicholas Davenport, a financier-journalist who worked closely with John Maynard Keynes for many years. In his 1964 book, *The Split Society*, Davenport wrote:

> How to make people who possess no capital feel that they have a stake in the country is an awkward political problem. As long as they suspect that the nation is being run in the interests of the finance-capitalists—the 2 percent of the population who own half the wealth of the nation—they will always feel alienated and at times incensed. The Labour attempt to bring about a wider distribution of capital through nationalisation was futile. Their whole socialisation programme tended to make the rich richer. And it brought no uplift in the worker's status. It was merely a change, as I have said, in management—and that of a peculiarly bureau-

cratic type....Labour should realise that a wider distribution of capital cannot be secured by nationalisation (which makes the rich more liquid) or by heavy discriminating taxation (which would merely drive the rich abroad) or by confiscation (which is rightly impossible in a democratic state). It can only be done by making poor people less poor and giving the mass of wage and salary earners a better chance to acquire some capital. [p. 169]

In his 1985 annual report to Great Britain's Wider Share Ownership Council, Chairman Edgar Palamountain said:

Now share ownership is fundamental to capitalism—at least in a free society—in two senses. First, because capitalism involves the ownership of the means of production, distribution and exchange by the people rather than by the State. Secondly, because share ownership, by involving people in the fortunes of the companies that create their wealth, fosters understanding of the system and acceptance of its merits. In an ideal free capitalist society, just about everyone would own shares, and the stability of the system would be assured.

That is the essence of our essay problem: How can we achieve an ideal free capitalist society in which just about everyone owns shares?

2c. Employee Ownership Distinguished from Universal Ownership

When you mention broadened capital ownership, most people think automatically of employee share ownership because that is the only established variety. While employee share ownership is an important step toward universal share ownership (USOP), it is necessary to distinguish between them to avoid obscuring the objective of the essay competition.

It is widely accepted that employees who have a financial interest in the outcome of their work apart from wages will be more strongly motivated and therefore more productive. I have found this to be true in my own business experience. Unfortunately, however, it is not possible to transform this well-accepted principle into a macroeconomic tool that can solve major economic problems and bring about social justice.

We shall consider employee ownership in Section 8 from the

standpoint of how it can be used as a foundation for a broader plan of universal ownership, and how USOP can act as a safety net for employee shares by providing convertibility, thus removing the "all eggs in one basket" defect of employee share ownership. At this point, it is only necessary to point out the reasons why employee share ownership cannot lead us directly to universal share ownership.

The main reason why employee ownership will not achieve our objectives is that it will not spread ownership of the productive assets of America or Great Britain broadly among the people. While most Britons and Americans are employed, the great majority would not gain any benefits from holding shares in the enterprises for which they work. The relatively few companies that remain successful and whose shares retain market value over a working lifespan of forty years, employ only a fraction of the populations of both the United States and Great Britain. The majority of people in both nations work for themselves, or for government agencies, or for entities that do not issue shares that are traded, or they do not work at all. Thus, employee ownership brings no benefits to the unemployed, the very poor, and those who are not fortunate enough to be long-term employees of continuously successful companies.

Furthermore, both in the United States and Great Britain, employee ownership has been facilitated by tax benefits, such as allowing employers to take tax deductions for issuing shares, and allowing employees to receive the shares, at least initially, without paying income taxes on their value. This amounts to a tax subsidy to the most fortunate sector of our societies: those who have steady employment with strong companies. To that extent, it decreases the funds available to help the disadvantaged sector: those not fortunate enough to be able to support themselves through such desirable jobs.

Any attempt to mandate universal employee share ownership would be of dubious value to the workers. It is difficult, if not impossible, to calculate the value of shares in closely-held companies, whose profits can be manipulated by changes in the salaries of top management or through various inventory practices. And since there is no market for such shares, an employee wishing to realize the benefits of the shares would have no one to sell them to.

Another pitfall of the employee ownership approach to universal capitalism is the specter of pension fund socialism. Employee pension funds already own collectively nearly half the shares of major American companies. But these pension funds do not give employees either legal ownership or control of any capital, nor do they enable employees to share in corporate profits. While pension fund money is parked in the stock of various companies from time to time, the worker-beneficiaries do not become shareholders, nor do they usually know in which companies their pension fund has been invested. On retirement, they simply receive monthly cash payments without ever becoming shareholders in any companies in which the pension fund may have been invested.

Their investments are usually administered by trustees (often bank officers) who are constrained by the "prudent man" principle to invest the funds in a manner that will best promote the financial security of retired employees. Until recently, the major American labor unions showed no interest in activating a true ownership role through their pension funds. But in 1980, the AFL-CIO adopted a new policy, dedicated to "social investment" of pension funds. In effect, they want to use pension funds to promote unionism and protect the jobs of their members. Although they do not yet have legal clearance around the "prudent man" obstacle, it is difficult to quarrel with their reasoning. Why should auto workers in Detroit have their pension money invested in the Sunbelt and in foreign companies that are destroying their jobs?

If social investment becomes the accepted practice, the investment is likely to be directed by labor leaders, and thus we will not escape from the overconcentration of financial power that characterizes our present system. The political ramifications of union involvement have already created problems in Canada, where pension fund socialism is more advanced. The Caisse de depot et placement du Quebec, known as the Caisse, is custodian of a group of Quebec pension funds, including the province's counterpart of Social Security. It has become the largest investor in the Canadian stock markets and is viewed as an ally of the Parti Quebecois, which came to power in 1976 on a platform advocating Quebec's separation from the Canadian confederation. Although the Caisse denies that it is a tool of the separatist party, its investment policy is worrying Canadian industrialists. It now owns about 10 percent of Canadian Pacific, the largest company in Canada. Canadian Pacific's management is concerned that as the Caisse increases its share ownership, it might abuse its power by forcing the company to favor operations and employees in Quebec. The Parti Quebecois itself has advocated state ownership of banks and large businesses.

If we allow labor unions to exercise control over large blocks of shares through pension funds, monumental conflicts of interest can occur. On the one hand, the unions would be representing current workers in wage negotiations and could, through voting control of the board of directors, push wages to the highest level. On the other hand, pension fund shares would decrease in value if wage increases led to a decrease in profits. And so it would go, around and around in a circle, until the union officials who wear both hats met themselves coming and going.

This dilemma is epitomized by the history of the Meidner Plan which has been under development in Sweden for more than a decade and is scheduled to be implemented during the late 1980s. In its original form, as designed by union economist Rudolf Meidner, it would require Swedish companies to pay 20 percent of their annual pre-tax profits into a special fund for the purchase of shares that would be issued to the labor unions—not to the workers, but to the unions themselves. Individual workers would not receive any share ownership or dividend payments. The shares would remain in the fund in collective form, and would always be controlled by the unions. Under this scheme, all significant businesses in Sweden would be majority-owned and controlled by the labor unions in less than twenty years.

The Meidner Plan has been an important issue in all Swedish elections since 1976. It has gone through numerous modifications, through which the Meidner label was dropped and the scheme was renamed "wage-earner funds." The question of who will own the shares is still up in the air, but the wage-earner funds have been activated and they are beginning to accumulate shares of Sweden's major businesses.

Similar schemes are now under study in Denmark, the Netherlands, and West Germany, and it is only a matter of time before such plans develop a constituency in the United States and Great Britain. Therefore, unless we devise a plan for broadening *individual* capital ownership, the insidious growth of pension fund socialism is likely to continue, paving the way for takeover of industry by union officials.

I hope you are convinced that you can't solve the essay problem through employee ownership. But let us not discard employee ownership, because it can play a very important role in opening the way to universal share ownership. Now let's look at some possible ways of making share ownership universal.

3.

THE KITTY HAWK MODEL OF USOP

The concept of universal capital ownership is at roughly the same stage now as were Orville and Wilbur Wright in December of 1903, when they were first attempting to pilot their 12-horsepower Flyer off the sand dunes near Kitty Hawk, North Carolina. Thus, the plan that will be explained in Section 3 is called the Kitty Hawk model of universal share ownership. You are free to use it as you wish. You can try to build on its strengths, cure its weaknesses, or ignore it and go off in an entirely different direction. I do suggest that you read it through carefully, because it is the only plan for achieving universal share ownership that has been studied and discussed in any detail.

We begin without any inherent obstacles in American or British capitalism that would prevent us from spreading capital ownership to all the people. There are no constitutional or statutory bars against this, nor are there any roadblocks in economic theory. Indeed, most economists will tell you that income distribution is a political rather than an economic question. If the legislature decides that it wants to distribute income through capital ownership rather than through welfare payments, it is free to do so. All that is needed is the political will to enact such legislation.

So, keep in mind that we are searching for a way to make our economic system consistent with our political democracy and with our concept of fairness, whether we call it social justice, the Golden Rule, or the product of Judeo-Christian heritage. As we go along, I will

17

describe the Kitty Hawk model in American terms, but please note that the principles involved are equally applicable to the British economy. Where British statistics differ, I shall try to enumerate the important British counterparts.

All Americans are eligible to become capitalists, and millions do own some shares of stock. But as we have seen, no more than 6 percent of Americans receive significant income from ownership of stock or other income-producing capital.

Yet there is a vast hidden reservoir of unowned wealth in this country, in the form of the *new capital* created each year by American business, which could provide a substantial amount of income for those Americans who presently own little or no capital. (Capital, in this context, does not refer to money, but rather to the plant and equipment that companies build or buy every year in order to increase production and generate more income.) The key aspect of this capital is that it is *self-liquidating*, meaning that it is designed to pay for itself out of the increased profits flowing from expanded production. So, for example, the cost of constructing a new automobile factory will, over time, be covered by the sale of new cars rolling off the factory's assembly line. This capital is designed to pay for itself regardless of who owns it—a wealthy investor, a struggling janitor, or a wooden Indian. (British readers here substitute the figurehead of *H.M.S. Bounty* for the wooden Indian.) In theory, then, anyone could become an owner of this new capital, *if* he or she were extended the necessary credit with which to purchase shares of stock in the companies creating the capital. (See Figure 1.)

In practice, however, credit for the purchase of shares or other income-producing capital is available only to those who already have savings or other holdings—those who can provide good collateral for loans, or in some way can make the credit power of business companies work for them.

In 1985, American business invested over $300 billion in the construction and purchase of new plant and equipment. (The projected total is $384.4 billion, but I have reduced it to $300 billion in order to focus on the expenditures of America's 2,000 largest companies, for reasons that will soon become apparent.) How is this new capital financed? Under our present system, 95 percent of these new capital expenditures are paid for by a combination of debt (loans or bonds) and internal funds (including retained earnings and investment tax credits). Only 5 percent is financed through the issuance of new common shares, and that 5 percent can only be purchased by those wealthy enough to secure credit or risk a cash investment. Essentially, then,

Capital investment pays for itself...

...no matter who owns it.

Long-term credit is the key.

Figure 1

this yearly pool of new capital is financed through devices that operate like a corporate plumbing system, ensuring that ownership of this new capital flows exclusively to the pinnacle class which already holds most of the nation's privately-owned shares. In Great Britain, the total annual business investment in new capital is about £24 billion, and the percentage paid for by issuance of shares is about the same as in the United States. (See Figure 2.)

As long as this corporate plumbing system remains intact, so too will the process of overconcentrating MOP ownership in the hands of a mere 6 percent of the population. And the remaining 94 percent will continue to be denied any real access to significant capital ownership, thus widening the gap between the haves and the have-nots. This process, according to Marx, is precisely what will lead to capitalism's demise. With the majority of the population lacking real purchasing power, particularly during inflationary times, there simply won't be enough customers for the goods and services produced by American and British business.

The corporate finance system pictured in Figure 2 is rigged to *absorb* most of the newly created capital into the company, providing automatic ownership for its present shareholders. Yet nobody questions this system. Obviously, the major shareholders who control corporate voting power have a interest in its maintenance. But what about the millions of Americans and Britons who don't own any shares—the noncapitalists? It would seem that they, too, view the system as immutable, accepting without question the notion that they cannot become shareholders if they don't have the necessary savings.

In addition to widening the wealth gap between owners and non-owners, this rigid system keeps billions of dollars bottled up in the companies for capital expenditures, thereby reducing the income available for mass consumption of the companies' products and services. Wealthy shareholders believe this practice serves their interests, for they would otherwise have to pay large income taxes on their substantial dividend income. They prefer to have this money remain in company coffers, where the value of their holdings can increase untaxed and without any additional investment on their part.

There is, however, nothing sacred or immutable about this plumbing system. No American Congress ever approved it; the Constitutional Convention did not even consider it; nor, to my knowledge, has any British Parliament ever sanctioned it. It is simply one method—and not necessarily the best method—of financing an industrial economy. In past prosperous times, when the economy was able to produce enough jobs and income to satisfy the expectations of most Americans

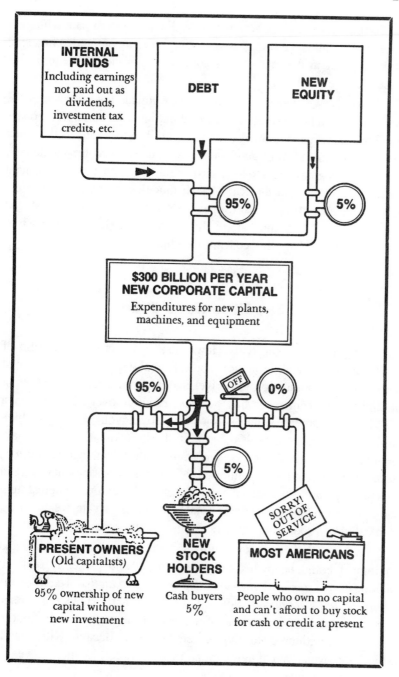

Figure 2. How capital expenditures (additions to the means of production) are financed under American capitalism

and Britons, there was no reason to question the system. But with faith in welfare capitalism eroding, we cannot cling to an outmoded financial plumbing system that perpetuates some of the principal inequities of laissez faire capitalism.

How can we change this? Do we dare invade the province of the capitalist and tinker with the system of creating new capital? To bolster our courage, let us look once again at Figure 1, which tells us that even the wooden Indians and figureheads among us can become capitalists, if only we can gain access to long-term credit. Now back to the financial plumbing system, and the Kitty Hawk model. (In previous writings, I have referred to this plan as ''SuperStock,'' but I have been persuaded to retreat to the more modest appellation of Kitty Hawk, leaving it to you essayists to bring this concept into the superlative class.)

The Kitty Hawk Plan

The purpose of the Kitty Hawk plan is to spread ownership of newly formed capital throughout society, enabling the noncapitalist 94 percent of our population to derive income from *direct participation* in capitalism. Remember that business requires over $300 billion a year for new capital, which is not owned by anyone now and which is projected to pay for itself regardless of who owns it. Over the next generation (roughly 20 years), according to the Brookings Institution, *Business Week*, and other authoritative sources, American new capital expenditures are expected to total at least *$5 trillion*. (Interestingly enough, that happens to be the total amount of private wealth, i.e., ownership of productive capital, in this country today.)

Imagine, then, the result if this $5 trillion worth of new plant and equipment could be owned solely by those who presently own no capital: *in one generation, ownership of the productive wealth of the nation could be equalized*. Not only would the Kitty Hawk plan create a more equitable distribution of income throughout society, but it would do so without disturbing present holdings. Because Kitty Hawk is based on ownership of *new* capital, there is no confiscation of wealth involved in the plan.

Can you imagine a better way of ensuring the survival of capitalism than by spreading the benefits of capital ownership to all Americans and Britons?

The New Plumbing System: Using Shares and Credit to Make Everyone A Capitalist

Kitty Hawk is designed to make stock ownership in America's 2,000 leading corporations available to everyone through a plumbing system that would funnel ownership of new capital directly to the 50 million households who now own little or no capital. To understand how it would work, let's go through it step by step, utilizing as a case in point the fictitious Peerless Pizza Parlors Corporation, which we shall imagine as one of the nation's 2,000 leading corporations. Let us assume that Peerless is building a new plant to meet increased demand for its new Possum Mark IV pizza oven. Thus, Peerless is creating $10 million worth of new capital *that is not presently owned by anyone* and that will *pay for itself* over time through the increased production and sale of pizza pies.

Under our present corporate plumbing system (Figure 2), Peerless financed such expansion primarily through internal funds and debt, which funneled ownership of 95 percent of the new capital into the bathtub of the current Peerless shareholders. There were some new shareholders, of course, but they were members of the elite class that had the savings or the credit needed to buy shares—the same group that owns the other 95 percent of this new capital. At the heart of the present system, then, is a mechanism for producing capital ownership that has been employed for centuries by wealthy individuals and businesses: *long-term credit*. At the heart of the new Kitty Hawk plumbing system is this same mechanism, but with one key difference: now long-term credit will be extended to the noncapitalists. Let's assume that you are one of the noncapitalists. Here's how you would become a capitalist:

(1) **Financing New Capital**: Under the new federal legislation adopting the Kitty Hawk plan, Peerless will not be allowed to pay for its plants through internal funds or debt. Rather, it will be required to finance its capital growth by issuing $10 million worth of a special type of stock, to be called USOP shares. This stock will not be available to the 6 percent of Americans who already own a substantial number of shares. Instead, you and the others who make up the 94 percent of the population that owns little or no capital will be able to acquire a given number of USOP shares. Now we come to the heart of the system: How do you pay for the USOP shares? You don't. A loan will be arranged to provide the money needed to pay Peerless for the stock, and eventually the stock will pay for itself out of its own earnings.

(2) **Credit**: The USOP legislation will establish a government-

guaranteed long-term loan program. In effect, *you* will be using the credit power of Peerless to acquire shares of its stock, just as Peerless now uses its credit power to acquire further capital ownership for its present shareholders. A bank loan of $10 million will be arranged, to provide Peerless with the entire cost of the new plant; Peerless will then issue $10 million worth of shares (at market value) when it receives the $10 million through the loan. But the loan will not be owed by you or by Peerless—it will be owed by the USOP fund. Until the loan has been repaid, the Peerless shares earmarked for your account will be held in escrow by the bank that made the $10 million loan.

(3) **Repayment**: The USOP legislation requires Peerless and the rest of the 2,000 participating corporations to pay out all their earnings as dividends, except those reserves actually needed to run the company. Thus, as Peerless begins to realize higher profits from the output of the pizza machines made in the new factory, these profits will be turned into higher dividends which are used to pay for the USOP shares issued to you. For a number of years, these dividends will be paid directly to the bank, until such time as it has recouped its $10 million loan, plus interest. Then you become the outright owner of your USOP shares, and you will receive all future dividends directly.

Thus, the new USOP plumbing system ensures that Peerless's $10 million worth of new capital is owned by millions of new capitalists—people who previously had no real access to capital ownership. (See Figure 3.)

I have over-simplified the Kitty Hawk plan to give you a bird's-eye view from the standpoint of a single company, Peerless Pizza. Actually, it is designed as a group plan, involving at the start America's 2,000 leading companies, such as General Motors, IBM, ATT, Xerox, and Exxon. These are the companies that every year create most of America's $384 billion of new capital, which I have rounded off to $300 billion in Figures 2 and 3 to represent the expenditures of these major companies. To pay for this capital, each company would issue shares of its stock at market value. These shares would be pooled in a sort of mutual fund or unit trust, with each company contributing to the pool the number of shares needed to pay for its new capital expenditures. Shares would be parceled out in bundles to those households eligible for the USOP program, with each USOP shareholder receiving shares in all 2,000 companies. So, for example, in a given year a USOP shareholder might receive a certificate of ownership for 9 shares of IBM, 12 shares of General Motors, 6 shares of Exxon, and so on, depending on how much each of these companies spent for new capital additions, the market value of each company's shares, and the

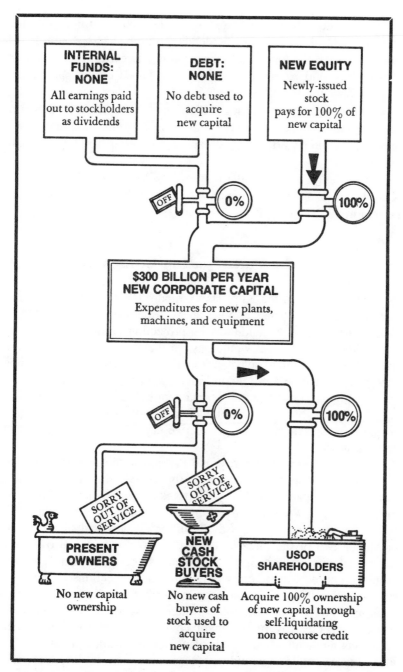

Figure 3. The Kitty Hawk Model Universal Share Ownership Plan: Financing capital expenditures through long-term credit, to spread MOP ownership throughout society and make income distribution equitable.

number of households participating in the plan. Earnings on these shares would be paid out as dividends, and the shares would be held in escrow until the loans had been repaid. Thereafter, ownership and dividends would be put directly into the hands of the participating households—the USOP shareholders. The program, which would be established through federal legislation and administered by a government agency, would continue for at least 20 years, producing in all about $5 trillion worth of new capital ownership for USOP shareholders.

Now let's zero in on the bottom-line questions: How might the Kitty Hawk plan be implemented? And what specific changes would be required?

3a. The Participating Companies

Participation in the Kitty Hawk model USOP would be open to approximately 2,000 major "blue-chip" American companies that can justify large capital expenditures by projecting future profits through which these expenditures would pay for themselves. In Great Britain, the participants could be selected from the 2,117 U.K. companies whose shares are traded on the London Stock Exchange. We're not going to be focusing on start-up ventures, small companies, or financially unstable operations, but on the profitable giants like IBM and ICI, in whose corporate assets most of the productive capital of the two nations is concentrated.

It would be up to Congress and Parliament to establish guidelines for selection of specific companies. In general, eligibility should be limited to companies with a solid track record of good returns on invested capital. We could, for example, begin the program with companies having annual sales of $100 million or more and showing a net profit for two of the three preceding years. We might also want to design safeguards: participating companies could be required to document proposed expenditures by submitting projections to the Securities and Exchange Commission, in much the same way they now have to justify capital additions to their bankers. But there would be no need to get the government involved in regulating capital investment or allocating funds. If the new plant did not work out for Peerless Pizza, its shareholders would suffer the same financial losses as under the present system. This would put the burden on the officers and directors of Peerless Pizza to make the same thorough studies and projections for the new plant that they would if they were borrowing the entire $10 million.

Pooling of the shares of 2,000 corporations would create a sort of mutual fund or unit trust, and would prevent any inequities in parceling out the shares. Every USOP shareholder would receive a piece of every participating company; there would be no big losers if one of the 2,000 participating companies did poorly. By the same token, there would be no big winners getting richer than others from the earnings of a particularly hot company. The goal is equitable distribution of both stock ownership and dividend income. Pooling would also simplify administration of the program. If individual USOP shareholders were allowed to select specific companies in which to own shares, the system would become chaotic. It would be almost impossible to sort out priorities and parcel out shares. The object is to give *all* Americans and Britons the chance to become capitalists, and the fastest and most effective way to meet this goal is to provide them with a diversified stock portfolio that produces a share of the profits of our leading companies.

Now for some questions you may wish to address in your essay.

Should the USOP legislation *require* the 2,000 leading American companies (and their counterparts in Great Britain) to issue USOP shares in payment for their new capital expenditures, or should participation be voluntary? Some observers think participation should be made mandatory, at least for a period of about twenty years, during which we could achieve equitable distribution of the nation's capital wealth. But others believe we should start it on a voluntary basis, giving tax incentives to those companies that participate voluntarily. Since USOP legislation would come much easier with support from the business community, it is worth trying to devise a method that would attract voluntary participation.

One way of doing this would be to eliminate the corporate income tax for participating companies. As we shall see in Section 3c, the corporate income tax is virtually eliminated on the USOP shares, so the full return earned on those shares could be paid out to the USOP shareholders; but that does not necessarily mean that the rest of the company's income should also be free from tax. As an incentive to attract companies to participate in USOP, it would probably be feasible to eliminate their corporate income tax entirely. Since the participating companies would be required to pay out all of their earnings as dividends, the Treasury would probably collect *more* money under such a program, because the dividends received by shareholders would be taxable, and the tax rate would probably be higher than the rate now paid by the companies on the profits they've retained to pay for capital additions.

Another way of encouraging voluntary participation would be to permit the USOP companies to advertise that they are Equal Ownership Companies. They might use an emblem similar to the blue eagle of the New Deal days to convey this message to consumers, who presumably would favor such companies when making buying decisions.

Another question: Whether USOP participation is voluntary or mandatory, how would the participating companies be selected? There are some guidelines above, but they would have to be spelled out more precisely in order to make certain we were including the major profitable entities whose shares could equalize the wealth of the nation without disrupting the economy.

Could we extend USOP to smaller companies? This is desirable in itself, in order to avoid any unfair advantage that the larger companies might gain by having exclusive access to the USOP funds. However, this would need to be balanced against the risks of loss inherent in new and small enterprises. You might address the question of how we could reconcile these two interests so as to avoid making USOP an anticompetitive force in the business world, and yet allow it to grow quickly by including more companies in the plan.

And here's one for you would-be loophole finders: Should USOP be extended to large mergers, acquisitions, and takeovers? Companies opposed to the USOP concept might try to evade it by taking over other companies instead of building new plants or installations of their own. We could plug that loophole by requiring the issuance of USOP shares in payment for acquisitions (takeovers) above a certain size. This would open to the USOP fund another huge pool of capital ownership, for in the United States the total amount paid for corporate acquisitions in 1984 was over $122 billion. (The comparable British total for 1984 was £5.47 billion.) Many of the large takeovers are financed by debt, including "junk bonds" that are of questionable economic value. Also, the "mergermania" outbreak resulted in retirement of about $100 billion of common stock in 1984, resulting in a net decline of at least $72 billion in the corporate equity base. Some commentators fear that this erosion of debt-equity ratio is a time bomb that may lead to massive business failures.

As you can see, the Kitty Hawk model of USOP is based on the capital expenditures of major companies, which I consider to be the engine of capitalism. You may want to consider other alternatives, such as using company profits as the reservoir for USOP. Please feel free to develop that theme, although I must warn you that you are going to wind up with a much smaller USOP if you use the exhaust fumes (profits) instead of the engine. In Section 3f below, we will discuss other potential reservoirs, such as profits and privatization.

In connection with use of the $300 billion annual capital expenditure as a reservoir for USOP, several people have questioned me about the treatment of capital expenditures that replace worn-out plants and equipment. Their point is that if Peerless Pizza, for example, plans to spend $10 million to construct a new plant in order to replace one that had cost $5 million, is it fair to deprive the present shareholders of the ownership of the new plant—or at least of ownership of half the new plant, as represented by the $5 million value of the old plant being replaced? My answer is that the shareholders would suffer no loss in this transaction, because they have already received the benefits of owning the old plant, in the form of increased earnings, dividends, or book value of their shares, as represented by the $5 million entered in the company's accounting records for depreciation. When Peerless undertakes to build a new plant for $10 million, it must raise this $10 million by either depleting its internal funds, borrowing the money, or issuing new shares. In any event, when it puts a new $10 million plant on the left side of its balance sheet as a new asset, there must be a corresponding $10 million liability, or reduction of assets, or increase in outstanding shares. Therefore, in my opinion, depreciation is not a relevant factor in designing or evaluating USOP. However, since this question has been raised, you may wish to address it in your essay. As always, you are free to disagree with my views, especially since I am not one of the judges of the essay competitions.

3b. The Government's Role in USOP

Implementation of USOP would, of course, require federal legislation and administration. Although Congress might choose to create a new government agency to run the program, it could be administered by the Treasury Department, the Department of Commerce, the Social Security Administration, or the Securities and Exchange Commission (SEC). The SEC might prove the wisest choice since it now regulates issuance of corporate stocks and bonds and would probably be involved anyway under existing laws.

Apart from administrative functions, the government's primary involvement in the USOP program would be to act as loan guarantor. Remember that in the Kitty Hawk model, USOP shareholders could not and would not actually pay for the stock, nor would they even have to sign notes for it. The government would step in, not with welfare handouts or grants, but with guarantees of the loans the banks would make to pay for USOP shares. These guarantees could be financed by loan insurance fees in a manner similar to the way the Federal Housing Agency and Federal Deposit Insurance Corporation operate now.

The risks involved in this plan, for both the banks and the government, would actually be quite minimal because USOP would be secured by the assets and earning power of our corporate giants. And because USOP would be essentially a portfolio of diversified stock, if any of the participating companies failed, the earnings of the remainder would be available to offset the losses. This is one of USOP's great innovations: creating a system of equitable income distribution based on the *strength* of capitalism—the ability of productive capital to pay for itself—rather than on the weaknesses inherent in government welfare handouts.

If you're wondering whether Congress has the power to order our 2,000 leading companies to issue stock in payment for their new capital additions, the answer is yes. Back in 1937, the U.S. Supreme Court decided that Congress, by virtue of its power to provide for the general welfare, could require companies to make Social Security contributions for their employees. Thus, if Congress decided that a national policy of capital ownership would promote the general welfare of the American people, it would have the constitutional power to enact the necessary legislation. Likewise, I have been assured by legal experts in the U.K. that there is no constitutional obstacle there.

There are also precedents for government guarantees of long-term credit. World War II veterans were able to secure government-guaranteed, low-interest home mortgages under the G.I. Bill of Rights. Most of these veterans did not have the savings or income to qualify for mortgages without this government subsidy. This program not only enabled millions of Americans to buy homes with no down payment, but it also helped to usher in one of our most prosperous economic periods. And even today the FHA guarantees banks against losses on loans made for the construction or purchase of homes. Certainly, if the government can guarantee loans for nonproductive items like homes, it should be able to guarantee loans for capital outlays that are both productive and self-liquidating.

This initial government involvement raises the question of whether USOP would lead to extensive government economic planning and possibly to a command economy like that of the socialist countries. This is a question you may want to treat in your essay. In my opinion, USOP need not involve us in any more extensive government planning than we have today. The planning and decision-making for capital additions can and should be done by each individual company. We might want to inject some sort of requirement for a projection that the capital additions will pay for themselves, but certainly such projections are required today by the boards of directors and finance committees of major companies before they incur large expenses for capital additions. To safeguard the public against erosion of the USOP fund, we might require that each participating company submit such a projection to a government agency such as the SEC. Again, this parallels what is done today in the private economy, because practically all securities issued by our large companies must be registered with the SEC beforehand.

We should also recognize that some degree of government participation is necessary in any successful industrial economy. Indeed, Henry Kissinger and other conservatives have urged the United States to copy the Japanese system, which is built on massive government planning and economic intervention. USOP would involve less government planning than the Japanese or the German system, and it would eventually *decrease* government intervention by reducing or eliminating welfare-state handouts that require huge bureaucracies.

This raises the question of what it would cost the government to put USOP into operation. In my opinion, it should cost nothing, because in the long run, USOP should actually save us money. It is designed to reduce government expenditures for Social Security, welfare, and other transfer payments, and it should enable us also to save some of the billions of dollars now spent on the hopeless task of job creation in an economic system that is designed to destroy jobs.

3c. Source and Repayment of Loans Used to Buy USOP Shares

As we saw in the Kitty Hawk model of USOP, the USOP shares issued by the 2,000 leading companies in payment for their capital additions would be financed by bank loans, guaranteed by the government. Then the shares would pay for themselves out of their own dividends. However, at the present time, American companies pay out only about 30 percent of their earnings as dividends; the other 70 percent is pumped back into the company in the form of retained earnings. Obviously, if USOP stock is to pay for itself in a reasonable time, the share of earnings paid out as dividends would have to be much greater than 30 percent. In fact, under the Kitty Hawk USOP, shareholders would receive the *full return* on invested capital. Participating companies would be required by law to pay out *all* of their earnings as dividends, except for the reserves actually needed to run the company. This would return companies to their original purpose: serving as instruments for distribution of profits to their shareholders. (See *Encounter* magazine, April 1985, p. 60, where British commentator Samuel Brittan says that the conservative economists F. A. Hayek and Milton Friedman also advocate full payout to improve efficiency and reduce management power relative to shareholder power; if all new investment had to be financed by new issues of bonds or shares, it would be more subject to market tests.) Indeed, under the new USOP system, companies would have no need for retained earnings anyway, since they would not be allowed to use them for capital outlays. Paying out these earnings as dividends would provide additional benefits as well. By pumping more income into the economy, we would be creating more customers, more taxpayers, and more production, which should be counter-inflationary.

How long might it take for USOP shares to pay for themselves? Anywhere from seven to fifteen years, depending on company performance (their rate of return on invested capital), interest rates, and the way the dividends are used. Let's take a closer look at these key factors.

Corporate Performance: Currently, most major American companies realize annual pretax profits of about 20 percent on their invested capital. If this entire 20 percent were paid out as dividends, USOP stock would repay its entire principal in five years; allowing for reasonable loan interest charges, repayment would take seven or eight years. But under our present system, some of these profits end up in government coffers in the form of corporate income tax payments. Clearly, if USOP shareholders are to receive the full pretax 20 percent earnings on their shares, major changes in the corporate income tax structure would be required, at least in regard to the USOP program. How might this be handled?

The simplest method would be to eliminate the corporate income tax entirely for those companies participating in USOP. Such an exemption would cost the Treasury some revenue, but the loss would be more than balanced by increases in personal income tax payments, since all shareholders, including USOP shareholders, would have to pay personal income tax on the dividends they receive. Currently, corporate taxes bring in less than 10 percent of U.S. tax revenues. Thanks to tax credits and loopholes, the average tax rate of our large companies is only about 20 percent, and many of the giants with profits in the $100 million range pay no federal taxes at all. It's quite likely, therefore, that the Treasury would collect *more* income tax revenue on dividends than it presently does through corporate taxes—since under USOP, what the companies wouldn't pay, the shareholders would. Furthermore, many economists believe it is impossible to tell who really pays the corporate income tax: The consumers, through higher prices? The company's employees, through lower wages? The company's suppliers, through lower prices? Or the shareholders, through lower profits and dividends?

Bear in mind as well that USOP would, in time, replace government transfer payments, such as Social Security and welfare. At present, with capital ownership concentrated in the hands of a small elite class, the government is forced to redistribute income, taxing the producers to provide income for the nonproducers (the unemployed, the disabled, the elderly). USOP would change this by putting capital ownership into the hands of those who now receive transfer payments. The dividends on USOP shares would replace the transfer payments, and government (federal, state, and local) would no longer need such massive tax revenues.

Elimination of the corporate income tax is not a new idea, but it has never gained popular support because it has always been viewed as a benefit for the rich. Under USOP, the benefits would go to the entire population. But we need not remove all corporate income taxes in order to implement USOP. We could, instead, simply allow the participating companies a tax deduction for their USOP dividend payments, in much the same way they now receive a tax deduction for interest payments. In that way, we could accomplish the objective of getting USOP paid for as quickly as possible by capturing the full pretax earnings on the new capital, while continuing to collect income taxes on the portion of company earnings not related to USOP.

One of the reasons American companies currently pay only 30 percent of their earnings as dividends is the double tax penalty. Before dividends can be paid out today, a company must pay taxes of up to 46 percent on its profits; then the stockholders must pay an additional personal income tax of up to 50 percent on dividends received. This tax structure encourages companies to hold back most of their earnings and use them for capital outlays. But if companies were no longer allowed to use accumulated earnings to pay for new capital, and if they were not taxed on earnings paid out as dividends, there would be no reason to hold back dividend payments.

Thus, if American corporate return on invested capital remained at the current 20 percent level, USOP would pay for itself in roughly seven years. Indeed, under USOP, earnings would be even higher since companies would be relieved of the interest charges they formerly had to pay on loans made for new capital outlays. (The Kitty Hawk model of USOP eliminates use of company debt to pay for capital additions.) If actual returns were less than 20 percent, repayment would of course have to be stretched over a longer period of time. Then, too, the repayment period would depend to an important degree on the amount of interest banks charged for USOP loans.

Interest Rates: If interest rates remain at the present oppressively high level (above l0 percent for home mortgages), that seven-year repayment goal isn't likely to be met. But there are several alternatives. The government could arrange for a lower interest rate on the financing of USOP shares; numerous similar government programs exist today. For example, sales of large airplanes to overseas customers by companies such as Boeing and McDonnell Douglas are subsidized by low-interest loans from the U.S. Export-Import Bank. This agency, which finances and promotes foreign trade, arranges for interest rates well below the prime market rate in order to spur trade and improve our balance of payments. Such low-interest loans have even been used for trade with communist nations. Other current federal loan guarantee programs, designed to spur the creation of jobs, have interest rates as low as 2 percent. Why not utilize the same sort of interest subsidy for a program designed to strengthen our economy and make all Americans capitalists? (If the banks would not go along with lower interest rates for government-guaranteed loans, the government could finance the program directly.)

Alternatively, we could simply accept the current high rates and finance USOP anyway, stretching repayment over a longer period, perhaps as much as 30 years, as is done now with many home mortgages.

Dividends: Repayment would also depend on the way dividends were allocated. The USOP shares would be held in escrow by the banks until the loans were repaid, and we could require all dividends to be paid directly to the banks during that period. While this would speed up repayment of the loans, it would also leave the USOP shareholders without any dividend income for at least seven years. If we found it desirable to start the flow of income to the USOP shareholders earlier, we might stretch out the repayment period to about l5 years and split the dividends in half. Fifty percent could go to the banks for repayment of loans and interest; the remainder could be paid directly to USOP shareholders as income.

In your essay, you may want to ponder this question of how USOP would pay for itself. Under the Kitty Hawk scenario, $5 trillion worth of shares of leading American companies would be owned by USOP shareholders about 20 years after the plan went into effect, and they would receive dividends of about $1 trillion per year. But the total profits of *all* American companies right now, even before taxes, does not even approach $1 trillion a year—so how can these figures be correct? Well, $5 trillion is the generally accepted figure for our total new capital requirement over the next 20 years. That money will be invested only in companies that can make a good case for a return of about 20 percent before taxes; otherwise, investors would be better off putting the funds into the money market. Therefore, this annual return of 20 percent should produce $1 trillion in dividends to USOP share-holders. Remember that USOP is based upon the *future growth* of the American economy (stretching into the twenty-first century) and nei-ther disturbs nor depends upon the return on presently owned capital. Also, company profits will be greatly increased by elimination of the massive interest payments now required under the present system, which uses company debt to pay for many capital additions.

In Great Britain, repayment would take somewhat longer because of the lower return on investment. Here I am going to avoid the risk of comparing apples and oranges, by leaving to British essayists the tasks of determining pretax return on investment; length of time re-quired for USOP dividends to repay the loans; total value of USOP shares issued over a period of 20 years; and total annual dividend income after 20 years. My own inquiries have produced enough con-flicting replies to convince me that further research is required to construct the British counterparts of the American USOP projections.

In sketching the Kitty Hawk scenario for USOP loans and their repayment, I have greatly simplified a rather complicated subject. You may well want to dig into that phase of USOP, carefully examining how the huge credits needed to finance the purchase of USOP shares could be created, managed, and repaid, without disrupting the banking system or causing inflationary pressures.

3d. Who Would Receive USOP Shares?

Now we come to the most controversial aspects of the Kitty Hawk scenario: the question of who would own the USOP shares, and in what proportions. Here I believe we may have a dichotomy between the American and British plans, because nearly all of the people with whom I have discussed this concept in Great Britain automatically assume that any such mass ownership plan would apply equally to all citizens, regardless of financial condition. Perhaps this is due to the British dislike for means-tested benefits, an attitude nurtured by more than forty years of difficulties in administration of the British welfare state. Perhaps Britons feel this way because relatively few (probably no more than half a million of them) receive substantial income from capital ownership, thus casting doubt on the need for selectivity.

My opinion is that even in Britain there is sufficient inequity in capital ownership and income to justify a means-tested policy. I believe that USOP is philosophically different enough from welfare payments so that the demeaning aspects can be managed more effectively when dealing with capital ownership. But that is up to you to treat in your essay, whether you are writing about the United States or Great Britain.

In the United States, we have some experience in achieving capital ownership through government allocation. During the 19th century, when land was our chief form of productive capital, the government allocated ownership of this capital to Americans through the Homestead Act, literally handing out 160 acres of land to anyone willing to settle it for five years. Obviously, when it comes to ownership of $5 trillion worth of productive capital in the form of company shares, we could not use the Homestead Act method of distribution.

There would be a lot of tough decisions for Congress to make in establishing the priorities for access to USOP—but they aren't nearly as tough as trying to make welfare capitalism work in a democracy where people have high expectations. Congress could establish some priorities and then have its Joint Economic Committee or other committees review them regularly. The priorities could be adjusted before any great damage was done, since USOP must be phased in over a period of at least seven years. But I suggest that Congress retain this function and not delegate it to an administrative agency. It's too important for that. It should remain under direct control of our most sensitive instrument of democracy.

We might start by excluding all households whose current net worth equals $100,000 or more. Or we could establish a point system for eligibility. Points could be awarded for low wages, lack of savings or capital ownership, willingness to work, physical disability, compliance with the law, and public service work. Points could be deducted for criminal violations, unwillingness to work, high wages, capital ownership above a certain level, and so on. Some weight would have to be given to the number of people in the household, and (as under the present system) there would have to be provisions for divorce or breakup of the household. First priority might be given to the working poor—the 20 million or more Americans whose income is below the poverty line even though they work. We might also consider giving special priority to the armed forces, the police and fire departments, nurses, and perhaps even politicians—people engaged in dangerous or demanding public service, which leaves them little opportunity to accumulate capital honestly. The idea is to make participation in USOP more attractive to public servants than bribery or featherbedding.

We would have to keep our Social Security and welfare programs alive, at least temporarily, to cover those who did not become eligible for USOP. But we should make the USOP route much more attractive, to encourage everyone to work out of the welfare system by becoming owners of the means of production.

There is no reason to make USOP available to those who commit crimes. Moreover, any USOP shareholders convicted of a crime should have to forfeit their holdings or turn them over to their victims. We need not repeat the fiasco of our Social Security system, where convicts who claimed physical or mental impairment resulting from their own criminal activities received disability benefits while in jail. Congress would also have to face the problem of those who have been convicted of crimes but have demonstrated that they deserve another chance.

The Homestead Act provides a useful precedent for confining ownership privileges to those who comply with the law. When Abraham Lincoln signed the act in 1862, it made land available only to American citizens who had never borne arms against the United States government or given aid and comfort to its enemies. Another precedent for awarding government benefits on the basis of valuable service and law-abiding conduct is the package of veterans' benefits made available under the G.I. Bill of Rights to those who served in the armed forces. The point is to use USOP to encourage compliance with the law; to bring citizens into the mainstream of society by convincing them they have more to gain by honest labor than criminal activities. At present, our system sends out a very different sort of message: by excluding millions of Americans from the mainstream benefits of capitalism, we are virtually inviting them to break the law and attack private property.

Once eligibility has been determined, how much could USOP shareholders actually expect to receive in stock and income? Remember that according to reliable projections, American business will create at least $5 trillion worth of new capital over the next 20 years. If that figure is divided among the 50 million households (out of the total of 86 million American households) who presently own little or no capital, each household would receive $100,000 worth of USOP shares. To express it more graphically:

$$\textbf{\$5 trillion divided by 50 million households} =$$
$$\frac{\$5,000,000,000,000}{50,000,000} = \$100,000 \textbf{ per household}$$

And at the current pretax return rate of 20 percent on invested capital, each household could expect to receive about $20,000 in dividends after their USOP shares have paid for themselves. Would a guaranteed yearly income of $20,000 impair the incentive to work? Perhaps. If so, we might build rewards into the system for those continuing to work. Remember too, that a lack of incentive to work is built into the present Social Security and welfare systems. If we could get USOP working to the point where it *does* threaten the work incentive, we would have the time and brains to solve that problem. Some of the potential solutions are discussed later in Section 4c.

In any event, we have to face the fact that we are entering the age of true automation, and there will not be work for everyone in the way we now think of work. If we develop a truly affluent society, many people will be able to work in research, the arts, the improvement of our public facilities and environment, or in occupations no one has dreamed of yet—*the work of humanity*. (This is discussed in Section 7.)

Adoption of USOP would force us to examine some basic questions: What kind of nation do we want to be? What kind of society can we afford? America was founded on the principle of political democracy, but we've never had economic democracy, nor have we ever dealt directly with the issue of wealth or ownership, either in the Constitution or in congressional legislation. There may be no easy answers, but surely the quest itself is worthwhile. And we can move slowly, particularly since USOP would have to be phased in over a period of at least seven years.

Provocative questions abound in this area. How should we handle inheritance? When a USOP shareholder dies, should his or her shares be inherited by the heirs, or should the shares go back into the USOP fund to be recirculated? This opens the more basic question of whether USOP shares should be allocated to households or individuals, and on exactly what basis. Economists and bureaucrats are comfortable with the term "households," but what is a household? (According to the U.S. Census Bureau, an average household consists of 2.7 people.) At a 1985 seminar on USOP at the University of Maryland, Anthropology Professor Nancie L. Gonzalez stopped me cold with that question. She pointed out that the components of a household are constantly changing, and that in dealing with long-term ownership the term is very confusing. She persuaded me that it would be much better to reduce USOP to the level of the individual, so that each person could determine his or her benefits and obligations. I have presented the overall plan in household terms to keep the figures in conformity with economics terminology, but for purposes of detailed analysis I think we should divide the "household" benefits by 2.7 to calculate the benefit per individual.

If we establish a means test based on present capital ownership and income, how would the figures be verified? Is this any more difficult than the determinations that must be made under the present welfare system? If you are alarmed at the difficulty of verifying the financial claims upon which the priorities would be based, please don't jump to the conclusion that it would be best to let everyone participate equally. This would greatly diminish the value of USOP (at least in the United States) as a potential means of equalizing the capital wealth of the nation in one generation. Why make 50 million disadvantaged noncapitalist households wait for another eight or ten years just so we can also confer ownership on the relatively rich 36 million households at the top of the totem pole? You may argue that Social Security pays benefits to the rich as well as the poor, but remember that the rich people receiving Social Security worked for it and had deductions taken out of their paychecks to fund future benefits. The same is not true of USOP shares.

How could a means test be imposed without demeaning the eligible people? Are there successful models in home ownership subsidy programs and other welfare-state programs that could be adapted to USOP?

If we wanted to use USOP to encourage socially desirable conduct, how could we establish the criteria?

What would happen when some USOP shareholders struck it rich in some other way—would they have to give up their USOP holdings, or would they stop accumulating USOP shares, or what? Remember that USOP is a gradual program and that it would take about 20 years for accumulation of the maximum benefit of about $100,000 worth of shares. Changes during that time could be taken into account through income tax returns or an annual reapplication for USOP shares to the agency administering the program.

3e.   The Nature of USOP Shares: Transferability, Voting Rights, and Basis of Dividends

Since we are setting out to design a new sysem of ownership, we are not necessarily bound by the present forms of ownership interests in large companies: shares of common stock, shares of preferred stock, bonds, debentures, notes, or the like. We are free to design an entirely new form of ownership, one that fits the purposes we are trying to accomplish through USOP. I believe that the basic purpose of USOP should be to bring about greater equity in income distribution. However, some people who support the principle of USOP do not agree with me. They believe USOP is capable of opening the way for greater political equality in addition to economic equality, and that the opportunity should be seized to pull off two bloodless revolutions at once.

This is a topic which you may well wish to address in your essay. As before, I shall give you my views, as well as some other opinions that may stimulate your thinking.

I believe that USOP shareholders should not be permitted to vote their shares, or transfer them (except possibly by inheritance). While these restrictions would deny the holders of USOP shares some of the advantages of earned or inherited wealth, the immediate reason for the plan is to heal our split society by using share ownership to make *income distribution* more equitable. No doubt the USOP shareholders would have a stronger feeling of paricipation in capitalism if they could vote and sell their shares or borrow against them, but I'm afraid the plan wouldn't work if we started out that way. If we could get it going to the point where it provides everyone a chance to reap the fruits of capital ownership through healthy dividend payments, that would be enough of a revolution to start off with.

USOP is not intended to change the control of corporations or to destroy the business skills it took us generations to develop. The USOP shareholders would not be receiving stock from their employers as compensation, and they would have no right to demand voting power simply because they participated in capital ownership through long-term financing arranged by the government. I see no reason to attempt two simultaneous revolutions by changing the management of our major companies as well as the ownership. Also, if USOP shares carried voting rights, proxies could be accumulated by unions or other organizations who might thereby take control of our major companies.

There is no reason why USOP shares must carry voting rights. Indeed, USOP need not use shares of stock at all. We could use something like a "capital ownership certificate" which would make the owner a capitalist but not a shareholder. It does not necessarily follow that the people who need more income are the ones whose votes should select and control company management.

If we wanted to make sure we were giving the USOP shareholders something valuable—securities yielding about 20 percent annual return on invested capital—we should not start out by endangering the position of the existing corporate management which makes such a return possible. Depriving USOP shareholders of the vote is not antidemocratic, because we are trying to establish democratic *ownership* of capital. We haven't reached the point of allowing the whole nation to vote in the election of company directors. That's another revolution, espoused by groups dedicated to changing the social responsibility and other functions of our business companies.

In his 1973 classic, *Small is Beautiful*, E. F. Schumacher recognized the importance of leaving company management free to conduct the company's business as in the past, even when the share ownership structure is changed for social purposes. He proposed that large companies be required to issue 50 percent of their shares to "the public hand," but went on to say:

> I am convinced that...nothing would be gained and a great deal lost if a public hand were to interfere with or restrict the freedom of action and the fullness of responsibility of the existing business managements. The "private" managers of the enterprises should therefore remain fully in charge....That is to say, the publicly-held shares would normally carry no voting rights but only the right to information and observation. [p. 287]

There are several ways in which USOP shareholders could be given the right of democratic participation in the companies whose shares they received through USOP. We could establish a national USOP Board of Trustees, who would be elected by the USOP shareholders. This Board of Trustees could administer the issuance of USOP shares according to the priorities established by Congress, and the collection and distribution of dividends. And, in order to afford USOP shareholders a measure of participation in management of our major companies, the USOP Board of Trustees could be empowered to elect or appoint one or more members of the board of directors of the 2,000 participating companies. (See also Section 12, USOP at the Local Level, which contains further ideas about voting power of USOP shareholders.)

Despite my feelings as stated above, you may want to consider whether USOP shareholders should be given the right to vote their shares directly, once the shares have been paid for. You may also wish to consider whether the proposed national USOP Board of Trustees should be given the power to elect directors of the participating companies in proportion to the shares held by the USOP fund, instead of limiting this right to the election of a minority of directors. Bear in mind that over a long period of time—a quarter-century or more—USOP would probably represent a majority of the shares of each of our 2,000 leading companies, assuming that shares of common stock were used.

As to nontransferability, USOP is designed to provide income which eventually would perform the functions of Social Security, welfare, and other transfer payments. Since USOP shares would be issued to a lot of people who have no experience in ownership of capital, we would have to put restrictions on the right to borrow against it or sell it, so that the recipients could neither squander it nor be cheated out of it. Here we can learn a lesson from the Homestead Act, under which the federal government gave out ownership of over 250 million acres of public land, only to see most of it bought up by commercial interests after the five-year residence requirement had been met.

As to the exact form of USOP shares, there are serious economic questions to be considered. In the Kitty Hawk model, shares of common stock are used for the sake of simplicity. But it probably would not be easy to keep track of exactly what portion of company earnings should be allocated to these USOP shares. Suppose, in our example, that the earnings from Peerless Pizza's new $10 million factory became commingled with profits or losses from other Peerless operations, and suppose that Peerless acquired other companies or was acquired itself in a merger or takeover: How would we continue to trace the amount of earnings that should be paid out as dividends on the USOP shares? And what happens after the new Peerless Pizza factory of 1985 becomes obsolete in 2005? The company no longer has the asset, but it has accumulated funds through depreciation allowances to build a new plant. How are these funds to be tracked in the corporate bag of assets? I am sure there are many creative solutions to this problem, and I hope this essay contest will bring forth some of them. One idea would be to use noncumulative preferred stock (called noncumulative preference shares in Great Britain). These shares would pay a fixed dividend when, as, and if earned by the company, and they would not necessarily require segregation of assets such as the new $10 million Peerless Pizza factory.

Another possibility is the recently developed asset-backed security or asset securitization. This practice started with the Government National Mortgage Association securities known as Ginnie Maes; they created a pool of mortgages against which securities could be issued to institutional investors and eventually to individual investors. Asset securitization has now been extended to the pooling of company receivables (accounts receivable), computer leases, and automobile loans. Can we use this principle for USOP?

Still another possibility is the new breed of unit investment trust, pioneered by the Americus Share Owner Service Corporation, that separates the dividend and price appreciation components of shares of major American companies. The Americus plan allows present shareholders of large companies (such as Exxon and ATT) to tender their shares to the Americus trust, through which the shareholders will receive an equal number of units in the trust, with each unit divided into securities called Primes and Scores, that may be bought and sold separately. Each holder of Primes, an acronym for Prescribed Right to Income and Maximum Equity, will receive cash dividends on the shares and a limited share of any price appreciation. Holders of Scores, or Special Claim on Residual Equity, will receive most of the price appreciation on the underlying company's shares during the five-year life of the trust.

A similar approach was taken by Merrill Lynch Capital Markets in its dual-purpose mutual funds, which permit investors to buy either income shares or capital appreciation shares in a pool of securities, and by Prudential-Bache securities in its dual-purpose commercial real estate securities program.

3f.   Other Potential Reservoirs

I have been able to identify six potential reservoirs which could be tapped to provide universal share ownership:

1. Capital additions of major companies, as featured in the Kitty Hawk model of USOP and as illustrated in Figure 3.

2. The purchase price of mergers, acquisitions and takeovers, discussed in Section 3a.

3. Privatization—government-owned assets and services that could be owned and operated privately.

4. Corporate profits.

5. A requirement for companies to issue new shares without any payment, the shares to be allocated to the new USOP shareholders.

6. An extension of the USOP principle beyond shares of major companies to other productive assets such as real estate.

We have already discussed the first two reservoirs. Some specific plans for using corporate profits and for requiring companies to issue new shares without consideration, are discussed in detail in Section 10 below. Here we will cover the third reservoir, privatization, and the sixth, extending the USOP principle beyond shares of major companies to other productive assets.

Privatization

Nationalization of major industries has not helped to bring economic equity to Great Britain. Indeed, nationalization favored the bought-out owners, who received huge sums for their moribund industries while everyone's taxes were increased to foot the bill. By and large, the nationalized industries have done poorly under British government management. But they would offer a perfect starting place for the British version of USOP. Nobody has any feeling of ownership about the nationalized companies—not the workers, the managers, nor the British public. The British coal mines, railways, and automobile factories have seen more than their share of strikes, even though they are owned by a government that is frequently controlled by the Labour Party.

Instead of returning the nationalized companies to private ownership, they could be owned by everyone in Britain. This might supply the missing link for British industry: the healing factor, the team spirit needed to create incentive for increased productivity.

Samuel Brittan, assistant editor and chief economic commentator for London's *Financial Times*, has been a strong advocate of denationalization, or privatization, of nationalized companies through distribution of shares to all British citizens. His arguments are summarized in his *Financial Times* column of September 20, 1984, entitled "The Case for Capital Ownership for All:"

> The concept of free distribution to all citizens of a right to a share in revenues from national assets originated in my case with North Sea oil. The privatisation programme of the present Government, provides another opportunity for the mass distribution of saleable rights to dividend income. The suggestion I made in *Financial Times* articles (and in more detail in *The Political Quarterly* of April-June 1984) was that instead of state assets being sold to investors, shares in them should be "given" to every adult citizen on a pro rata basis.
>
> It is only frank to admit that if the state assets are "given away" there will be less scope for cutting taxes than if they are sold (or more need to increase taxes if fiscal developments are adverse). Instead of obtaining tax cuts, citizens will instead have dividend payments on their denationalised shares. These dividend payments would have the following advantages over tax reductions:

(a) Distribution. Nationalised industry stock would initially be distributed equally to all citizens. Tax cuts inevitably benefit those who pay most taxes.

(b) Capitalisation. Even more important: holders of the new stock would be able to realise their assets in the market, or borrow on their strength, and thus have the benefits of wealth ownership. There is not, on the other hand, and could hardly be, a market in rights to hypothetical future tax cuts.

In contrast to both nationalisation and privatisation—which if carried out at "fair market prices" leaves the distribution of wealth unchanged—privatisation which takes the form of handing over shares to all citizens without payment does help make the distribution of capital assets less concentrated.

The main distasteful feature of investment or unearned income is that too few of us have it. Writers down the ages have sung the praises of a "modest competence," i.e., a private income, and the sense of independence it brings. It would be worth extending this undoubted privilege more widely. Popular ownership of shares in the formerly nationalised industries would only be a small step in shifting the distribution of capital ownership, but it would be a worthwhile start.

The one plausible objection to mass handover of state shares is that the amounts involved per family would be modest. My own estimate was that a family of two adults would have a stake worth £2,500 with dividend income approaching £150 (assuming a very slightly higher yield than on existing equities).

The North Sea oil stock, if it had come off, might have provided the same family with an annual income of £500 during the peak years of oil revenue and be worth perhaps £4,000. So the two schemes together would have been far from negligible; and this fact emphasises how important it is to seize any opportunity for mass ownership that arises.

While the United States has no exact counterpart of the British nationalized companies, it does have "national assets" that some American conservatives believe would be better operated by the private sector. This is the theme of *Privatizing Federal Spending: A Strategy to Eliminate the Deficit* by Stuart M. Butler, director of domestic policy studies at the Heritage Foundation in Washington, D.C. Some of Mr. Butler's leading candidates for privatization are the postal service, public housing, the Amtrak railroad system, and the air traffic control system.

There are two main choices in privatization. The government can sell the assets in question to private investors, thus increasing the cash flow of the treasury; or the government can give the shares away to all of its citizens. The first course, chosen by Margaret Thatcher, is popular with the London financial market, but unpopular with many Britons, who feel that they already owned the North Sea oil and British Telecom (the telephone company). Theoretically, of course, all the British people benefited from the cash sale of these assets, since it either reduced the government deficit or reduced the amount of taxes that the British government would need to levy in order to maintain its services. But wouldn't it have been a much more direct benefit to the British people to receive shares directly in these companies, so that each citizen would benefit equally?

In its first six years in office, the Thatcher government returned twelve major state-owned companies to the private sector, including British Aerospace, National Freight Company, Cable and Wireless, Amersham International, Associated British Ports, Brit Oil, Enterprise Oil, Jaguar cars, and British Telecom. Together these companies represent more than 20 percent of nationalized industry, measured by the number of employees or by output. Slated for sale in the near future are British Gas, British Airways, the Royal Ordinance factories, and the British government's remaining 48 percent shareholding in Brit Oil. Therefore, unless something is done fairly soon, Mrs. Thatcher will have sold off all of the income-producing assets of the nationalized companies, leaving only a few lemons for possible share distribution to the citizenry.

Canada's third largest province, British Columbia, furnishes a model for the use of USOP in privatizing business. The New Democratic Party held office in British Columbia from 1972 to 1975, during which it bought substantial shares of several leading local natural resource companies. But in 1975, British Columbia voters, disenchanted with the Socialist bent of the New Democratic Party, voted them out and elected as prime minister William R. Bennett, leader of the Social Credit Party and the millionaire son of a previous British Columbia prime minister, known as a champion of free enterprise. Bennett decided to privatize the natural resource companies owned by the province, but instead of selling off the shares to the lucky few who had the savings to pay for them, he came up with a new idea. He organized British Columbia Resources Investment Corporation (BRIC) to hold the shares of the natural resource companies, and he pushed through legislation that provided for distribution of 80 percent of its shares on an equal basis to every adult citizen of British Columbia. Each resident received five shares. In addition, BRIC offered shares for sale to the public, which scooped them up enthusiastically. The BRIC charter does not permit any person or company to own more than 1 percent of the total shares of BRIC, except that pension funds may own up to 3 percent.

BRIC took over government-owned assets worth several hundred million dollars, and it raised nearly $500 million through sales of additional shares. Of special significance to me is the fact that Premier Bennett is known as a pro-business conservative. He seized the opportunity to make every citizen of his province a capitalist. Historically, British Columbia has experienced bitter class divisions going back to the early part of the century when radical labor leaders such as Joe Hill and Big Bill Haywood were organizing workers. Even today, British Columbia has a higher proportion of unionized workers than any other Canadian province.

The gift of five shares to each eligible resident of British Columbia went to some 2.4 million Canadian citizens who resided in British Columbia for at least the immediately preceding twelve months. Application forms were handled by credit unions, banks, investment dealers, trust companies, and other financial institutions. All those eligible for free common shares were also permitted to buy up to 5,000 shares at $6 per share, the public offering price fixed in June 1979. The initial Board of Directors included the chairman of Okanagan Helocopters, Ltd.; chairman of a bank; chairman of a development corporation; chairman of a department store chain; chairman of a tractor manufacturing company; and a barrister-solicitor. There are no government representatives on the board or in management.

In his announcement on the distribution of free shares on January 11, 1979, Premier Bennett said:

> It is a unique, once-in-a-lifetime opportunity for the greatest number of people to become owners, not tenants in our land....We want people to be able to see and feel their ownership in the form of tangible share certificates. This share ownership will bring home to everyone, and particularly those who have never owned shares before, the value of ownership which can pay rich personal dividends....Too often we hear that only the wealthy and privileged have a chance to enjoy such an opportunity. Now every resident of our province has a chance to get a piece of the action.

The prospectus states, "In order to significantly reduce registration costs, voting and registration rights are restricted to share holdings of 100 shares or more." This means that the free shares, while common shares, do not have voting power, since each recipient got only five shares. However, all shares are freely transferable. The shares that were distributed free to all citizens are called "bearer" shares, and can be transferred like bearer bonds.

In 1984, BRIC established a Shareholder Liaison Committee, chosen from a list of more than 1700 names nominated by BRIC shareholders. The Committee visits company operations and meets with company management at least twice a year, at which time the Committee members report the concerns and questions of shareholders. This committee could furnish a model for the national USOP Board of Trustees suggested in Section 3e earlier.

Like most companies whose income is dependent on sales of coal, forest products, oil and gas, BRIC has had its ups and downs in recent years. But BRIC has managed to avoid major losses and has maintained profitable operations, while increasing its revenues beyond $1 billion and building the book value of its assets to $2.4 billion in 1984. (For further information on BRIC, write to British Columbia Resources Investment Corp., 1176 West Georgia St., Vancouver, B.C. V6E 4B9, Canada.)

Extending USOP Beyond Stock,
to Real Estate and Other Productive Assets

Can the USOP principle be extended beyond ownership of shares in 2,000 large companies? I chose them as the main reservoir of USOP because their shares have a readily ascertainable value and their history of earnings is consistent enough to provide the basis for USOP shares to pay for themselves out of their own earnings. Of course, the broader scope we can give to USOP, the more attractive the program will be.

In your essay, you might consider the shares of smaller publicly traded companies that do not have consistent earnings records; companies whose shares are not publicly traded but nevertheless are potentially or actually profitable; enterprises that are not organized in the corporate form, such as partnerships and individual proprietorships; personal property with a potential for capital appreciation, such as paintings and other collectibles; and, perhaps the greatest potential profit area of all, income-producing real estate.

Little has been written about this in the United States. In Great Britain, the idea has been mentioned by Professor James Meade and Professor Ronald Dore. In his article, "Full Employment, New Technologies and the Distribution of Income" (*Journal of Social Policy*, Vol. 13, Part 2, April 1984), Professor James Meade makes this statement:

Surely there must be a better way of organizing our institutions so that new technologies which could enable everyone to have a higher standard of living than before will not threaten to lead to either of these disastrous situations. My answer would be to attempt to devise wage-setting institutions which would allow the real wage rate to fall to the extent necessary to provide employment opportunities to all who sought them, but to combine this with fiscal and other institutions which ensured that directly or indirectly everyone enjoyed a fair share of the profits earned on the robots, computers, and tapes *and indeed on property in general*. (pp. 139-40; emphasis supplied)

In the 1985 T.H. Marshall Memorial Lecture, Professor Ronald Dore took up Professor Meade's idea of a social dividend, and suggested that in addition to corporate profits, the reservoir could include a share in "ownership title to real estate and art objects valued over a certain sum, that share to be realized whenever the item changes hands." Professor Dore's plan is considered in more detail in Section 10 below.

4.

THE KITTY HAWK MODEL: OVERALL EFFECTS ON ECONOMY AND SOCIETY

Let us now examine the overall effects of the Kitty Hawk model of USOP on the American and British economies and societies. First, the United States.

The changes required to implement USOP would be less radical than the U.S. Income Tax Law of 1913 and the U.S. Social Security Law of 1934; the benefits to our society, however, would be far more profound. By providing all American households with yearly dividends of up to $20,000 we could create the new customers and provide the massive infusion of purchasing power needed to match our huge productive capacity. Increased production would, in turn, help to reduce inflation, as would the eventual replacement of all social welfare transfer payments with the income earned by investment in productive capital.

Of course, these changes would not occur overnight, but the very prospect of making American capitalism work for everyone should start the juices flowing. In fact, the mere announcement of the initiative could provide an enormous psychological boost for our society. Right now, according to many professional economists, fear itself impedes economic recovery. Inflation is accelerated by the expectation that it will continue and by the perception that the government has no plan to stop it except by creating recessions. Many wage and price increases, for example, are based not on present needs, but on the expectation of prolonged inflation. Thus, fear and pessimism feed what amounts to a self-fulfilling prophecy. Leading economists all the way back to Adam Smith, Alfred Marshall, and John Maynard Keynes have recognized the strong influence of emotional and psychological factors on the economy. Marshall, Keynes' mentor, ascribed many economic phenomena to human nature. Keynes himself wrote in his 1936 classic *General Theory*:

> There is the instability due to the characteristic of human nature that a large proportion of our positive activities depend on spontaneous optimism rather than on a mathematical expectation, whether moral or hedonistic or economic....Thus if the animal spirits are dimmed and the spontaneous optimism falters, leaving us to depend on nothing but a mathematical expectation, enterprise will fade and die—though fears of loss may have a basis no more reasonable than hopes of profit had before. [pp. 161-2]

In 1982, Professor Shlomo Maital expressed a similar theme in his book *Minds, Markets, Money*, concluding that "minds pervade markets." It would seem, therefore, that USOP would provide the vital ingredient missing from the standard remedies for our economic malaise: a credible basis for optimism.

It would be difficult to imagine a policy more suitable for creating national unity and improving the American morale. It is consistent with America's greatest traditions, both liberal and conservative. It is conservative in that it would reduce taxes, eventually eliminate transfer payments, reduce the budget deficit, and check the growth of government bureaucracy, while preserving private ownership and existing financial institutions, and supporting business. It is liberal because it does more for the ordinary individual than all of the government welfare schemes ever dreamed up. And it would enable Americans to achieve economic independence without relying on welfare.

For the first time, our economic system would mirror our system of political democracy, and we would be affluent enough to deal with problems like poverty, pollution, health care, and crime. We would no longer have to feel guilty about an undemocratic, inequitable capitalist system, so we could begin to enforce the criminal law in good conscience.

The inequities of our capitalist system, in fact, are important causes of crime and social unrest. I am not one of those who would suspend criminal laws until we have created a utopia with equal opportunity and wealth for all. If we let crime proliferate because criminals are poor—or for any other reason—we'll never survive. But there is no doubt that people in the poorest sector of the economy, the sector which breeds most of our criminals, will continue to feel alienated as long as they remain shut out of the economic system. Our jails are already overflowing, and we are drifting dangerously toward accepting unemployment rates of 20 to 40 percent among the people who commit most of our violent crimes. Yet what can we do now but hand out welfare, even though we know that government handouts do not breed respect for the law?

Now consider USOP's impact on this critical problem. By giving everyone the opportunity to become part of the establishment, we would take a long step toward removing a major cause of crime. There would be no basis for anyone to feel exploited or left out of the system. There would still be criminals, of course, but few enough to be controlled by reasonable police action. Remember, too, that we can encourage the highest standards of behavior and morality by closing the plan to those who commit crimes. With all households assured of a sizeable income, few people would have logical reasons to take the risks of imprisonment and loss of USOP dividends.

Nigel Lawson, Chancellor of the Exchequer, giving the Maurice Macmillan Memorial Lecture in the House of Commons on June 11, 1985, said:

> We seek to create a society in which enterprise and responsibility flourish side by side. In which public ownership means what it says: ownership by tens of millions of individual members of the public...a society in which the sterile "them and us mentality" is replaced by a sense of common interest and shared purpose.

The potential overall benefits to the British economy and society are similar to those in the United States. Beyond these is the basic problem of English society: "us vs. them," the class system that persists despite many attempted political, social, and economic reforms. With every Briton a capital-owning first-class citizen, the confrontation factor would be greatly reduced if not eliminated over time. Samuel Brittan has summarized this potential in a 1985 article, "Thatcherism and Beyond," in *Encounter* magazine, April 1985:

> The trouble with economic policies pursued by European Governments—most of which are "Thatcherite" without the name—is that they represent the reaction of the 1970s to the mistakes of the 1960s. The trouble with most of their critics is that they simply want to put the clock back to the 1960s and return to "reflation,"

incomes policy, and yet higher public spending...as if nothing
had happened. What is still missing is a policy attuned to the
needs of the 1980s and '90s.

With hindsight it can be seen that both the Keynesian Revolution
and the Monetarist Counter-Revolution were "dazzling digres-
sions" from the main problem. The defect they both had in common was that they thought they could make a successful detour
around the labour market—the market which was malfunction-
ing—by skilful adjustments of financial aggregates. An attack on
the high unemployment that has infested European capitalism will
need to tackle it at its source—which is the wage system and the
ownership of capital. [p. 61]

4a. Effects on Inflation

One of the main causes of our recurring inflation is the attempt
to support our population through wages and welfare. The false promise
of full employment, which cannot be realized in this mechanized age,
creates inflationary pressures on our politicians. So they hand out more
welfare in place of the nonexistent jobs. As taxes increase to feed the
growing appetite of welfare and Social Security programs, cost-of-
living salary raises become a necessity. As a result, we pay people
more money for doing the same amount of work, which creates strong
inflationary pressure. USOP, however, would relieve much of this
pressure by eventually assuming the functions of Social Security and
welfare, thus making our economy less dependent on wage increases.
Workers who have an ownership stake in the means of production and
are receiving a second income from that ownership would have less
need to press for wage increases.

What's more, USOP would make it easier to swallow some of
the harsh medicine needed to halt inflation, such as raising the Social
Security eligibility age to 67 or 68, and implementing government
spending limits. USOP would eliminate the need for the "us against
them" philosophy. Policies that do not work under welfare capitalism
or socialism, such as public works programs and wage-price controls,
should become workable. In the split society of welfare capitalism,
such government policies are doomed before they are implemented,
with powerful special interest groups poised to defeat the legislation
required to make such programs effective. With the nation united by
a fairer distribution of MOP ownership, we could put the necessary
teeth into such legislation. Certainly, wage and price controls would

be more palatable if enacted by a united society such as we had during World War II, when the controls worked quite well.

Perhaps we might finally adopt a Tax-Based Incomes Policy (TIP), an idea proposed by the late Professor Sidney Weintraub of the Wharton School which has been endorsed by both Democrats and Republicans but never put into effect. TIP is intended to curb inflation via tax credits, without causing recession. So, for example, if we wanted to hold price increases to 3 percent per year, we could offer producers tax credits for meeting that goal. And workers willing to accept wage increases of 3 percent or less could receive an incentive in the form of similar tax credits. Alternatively, workers or producers exceeding these limits might be subject to tax penalties. Despite the obvious merits of TIP, it has never come close to enactment because the "us against them" factor in our present system makes it virtually impossible to achieve effective legislation.

Now to the bottom-line question: Is the Kitty Hawk model of USOP itself inflationary? The $300 billion worth of credit needed to finance the purchase of USOP shares might appear to be inflationary, since creating massive amounts of new credit is virtually the same thing as printing money. However, there is no reason why this credit feature has to be inflationary.

Actually, the loans used to finance USOP shares would not create entirely new credit demands, since our corporations are already borrowing huge sums to finance capital expenditures and acquisitions of other companies. Moreover, by doing away with transfer payments, USOP eventually would reduce the need for massive government borrowing to finance budget deficits, a process that raises interest rates and fuels inflation. In this respect USOP would have a counterinflationary effect.

When Senator Mike Gravel held a seminar on his Full-Return Stock Plan (described in Section 6 below) at the Brookings Institution in 1977, one of the questions raised was the inflationary effect of this credit scheme. According to Professor Lawrence D. Klein, the Nobel Prize-winning Wharton economist who chaired the meeting, the expansion of credit to finance the stock purchase program would not be inflationary if the money was used for investment that raises productivity. That, of course, is precisely where the USOP money would go: to pay for new plants and equipment. Klein also noted that wage demands were likely to be more moderate if workers were stockholders, since they would benefit from lower labor costs which would increase profits and dividends to shareholders. (See Appendix A for a summary of the meeting.)

Nevertheless, if the creation of credit for the Kitty Hawk USOP model did prove inflationary, we could implement the plan gradually. Instead of committing the entire $300 billion in new capital during the first year, we might begin with only a quarter or half of that amount. The important thing is to get started in the right direction. In fact, if we cut the entire plan in half, we'd still wind up with a much stronger economy than we have today.

In the event that implementation of USOP strained our credit facilities, we could consider setting priorities for access to credit. The point here is that credit used to pay for USOP shares would make our economy work better and bring us closer to economic justice, whereas loans for such transactions as one huge company taking over another are not really productive; these could be given a lower priority or cut off entirely until the credit strain was ended.

In considering the inflationary potential of USOP, we should calculate the costs of carrying out the plan, for if it involved large costs to the government, it could be as inflationary as welfare capitalism. But as we have seen, USOP differs from welfare capitalism in that it ties benefits to profits—the profits and dividends actually produced by capitalism, which all of us, working together, can create by tapping the inherent strength of the system. Therefore, USOP should prove far less costly than welfare capitalism. It could eventually reduce or eliminate government expenditures for Social Security and welfare.

The administrative costs of USOP would be negligible, probably far below the present costs of welfare and Social Security administration. And the risks involved in government loan guarantees would be minuscule. Today the government makes credit guarantees amounting to hundreds of billions of dollars for programs that cannot do half as much good as USOP. And what about the many large guarantees our government has made with very high risks of default, such as to Chrysler and New York City? USOP loan guarantees would not be nearly as risky. They would be backed by strong security: the shares of our 2,000 leading corporations. Even if some of them went into bankruptcy, the others would back up the loans. Don't forget, USOP is based on the strongest segment of our economy.

Thus, USOP should, in fact, pay for itself many times over. It would be able to pay its own costs of administration and save us many billions of dollars each year from our present government expenditures.

In the United Kingdom, the dynamics of the Kitty Hawk model and inflation would be substantially similar to those in the United States.

4b. Effects on Income Taxes

Both the British and American income tax systems have become too complex for most people (including judges and lawyers) to understand. One of the main reasons for this complexity is that both tax systems have been used to implement a broad array of social policy goals. If the tax system did not have to be used to support the welfare state, there would be a much better chance of simplifying it and making it more equitable.

Both systems are inequitable because they allow the rich to take advantage of loopholes and tax shelters, while imposing disproportionate burdens on taxpayers at the lower end of the income scale. There is broad agreement across the political spectrum that the tax system should be simplified and that the rate could be cut substantially without decreasing revenues if most deductions were eliminated. But as long as transfer payments are needed to keep capitalism afloat, it will be difficult to muster a legislative consensus for true tax reform.

Since USOP would do away with the need for most transfer payments that come from tax revenues, our social policy goals could be accomplished without having to filter the money through our horrendous tax system. Thus we could simplify the tax system, reducing rates across the board and eliminating the inequitable loopholes. Indeed, one of the main features of the Kitty Hawk USOP model is elimination of the corporate income tax, which has become inequitable in its own field because many large profitable companies pay little or no tax while others pay rates up to 45 percent in the United States and 40 percent in the United Kingdom. The Kitty Hawk USOP model would eliminate all these inequities and would require that earnings be paid out as dividends, which would be taxable in the hands of the recipients, probably at higher rates than those paid by the companies on their earnings.

4c. Effects on Employment, Work Incentive, and the Weitzman Plan

In an increasingly automated age, no plan appears capable of producing full employment. USOP, however, represents our best hope of reducing current unemployment levels. By supplying additional purchasing power and sorely needed funds for new product research and development, it would certainly create new jobs. Even more important, once USOP is adopted, unemployment would be less of a problem because people would receive a substantial dividend income whether or not they worked.

This of course raises another key question: Would the work incentive prevail if people can live well without working very hard or perhaps without working at all? I don't believe capital ownership automatically diminishes a person's willingness to work. Many people who own substantial amounts of capital continue to work; indeed, many work harder than those who own no capital. Perhaps the key element is *participation*. Owners enjoy working within a system that offers them full participation, but workers who are shut out of ownership rarely develop the same enthusiasm for their jobs. It's quite possible, therefore, that the prospect of full participation offered by USOP would strengthen, rather than weaken, the work incentive. Furthermore, any large-scale erosion of the work incentive is likely to be reflected in decreased earnings and lower dividends to USOP shareholders, which should inspire them to work.

But even if this did not prove to be true, the problem is not insurmountable. We could, for example, make larger blocks of stock available to able-bodied people who continue to work. For most, the opportunity to augment spendable income through working should be incentive enough, especially when inflation cheapens the dollar. In 1977, the University of Michigan Survey Research Center found that 75 percent of Americans would prefer to continue working even if they could live comfortably without working for the rest of their lives. Similar findings were made by Herbert McClosky and John Zaller, published in their 1984 book, *The American Ethos: Public Attitudes Toward Capitalism and Democracy*, pp. 108-110.

But no matter how we decide to solve this problem, USOP offers us a unique opportunity to start fresh, avoiding the disincentives that exist in our present welfare programs, and creating new work incentives. Indeed, whatever the problems of administering USOP, they are not likely to be worse than the problems of welfare capitalism. Moreover, we Americans are renowned for solving management problems. Given a more logical and equitable system like USOP, we can quickly become experts at using its new powers to reward those who contribute as much as they can to our society.

Not everyone enjoys work for its own sake—but just about everyone loves ownership. And if ownership requires work and other socially desirable behavior, it will be forthcoming.

While work incentive might be something of a problem during the early stages of USOP, we would have to make an even more difficult adjustment in our basic concept of working. Even if USOP stimulated the economy with fresh purchasing power, there probably wouldn't be enough paid employment to go around. Some states have already adopted "work sharing" to enable companies to shorten the work week and thereby avoid layoffs. In those states, when a company cuts its work force by 20 percent, for example, it does not lay off 20 percent of its employees, but instead reduces the work week to four days; for the fifth day, workers receive prorated unemployment payments from the state. These changes in work patterns are not likely to disappear. In fact, when the robots proliferate, the four-day week and then the three-day week will become the norm, and people will retire at earlier ages.

USOP could facilitate these changes. Right now, most people view work-week cutbacks and early retirement with alarm because such measures signal a loss in spendable income. But if those losses were made up by income from USOP dividends, we would create an ideal bridge to the new age of the shorter work-week. And that age must come, if only because a shorter week, early retirement, job-sharing and similar measures will enable us to reduce unemployment by spreading available work more evenly throughout the work force. Under our present system, these "future shock" changes are likely to cause great resistance and social upheaval. But if workers could count on a substantial capitalist income, the transition to new employment patterns could be both peaceful and productive.

All of these changes could, in turn, offer us exciting opportunities to expand our culture and improve the quality of our lives. In generations to come, freed from the crushing burden of economic insecurity, millions of people would be able to engage in the work of humanity. For example, there is pollution control, which is the work of both industry and humanity. If industry expands as I believe it would under USOP, it would take plenty of humanitarian work to preserve our environment and resources. And for the first time, we'd have the kind of affluent society that can deal with these and other problems. Every ghetto and slum, every decaying urban waterpipe and sewage system, every polluted river, could become a golden opportunity instead of a dead weight. We already have the brains, the computers, the technology. USOP would allow us to reap the full benefits these resources can provide. (In Section 7 below, the work of humanity is discussed from the standpoint of enabling USOP shareholders to earn their shares.)

USOP and The Weitzman "Share Economy"

In his 1984 book, *The Share Economy—Conquering Stagflation*, M.I.T. economics professor Martin Weitzman suggests that U.S.

business abandon the practice of paying fixed wages and instead compensate workers in relation to their employers' revenues or profits. He attributes stagflation to the universal practice of paying employees fixed wages. When sales decrease during recessions, companies have difficulty reducing prices because they often cannot reduce wages and indeed sometimes even must increase them. Therefore, business managers choose instead to cut production and lay off employees. Thus, even as wages go up, unemployment rises and inflation persists. Weitzman suggests that if workers agreed to accept a share of the company's revenues or profits—say, two-thirds—then when revenues dipped during a slump, workers' income would drop accordingly and the firm could then reduce prices in order to revive sales. Because all workers would take a temporary cut, no one would have to be laid off, and the burden of the recession would be spread throughout the whole work force.

Weitzman also claims that in such a share system, the company would have more incentive to hire new employees during better times. The new workers would help increase production when sales were climbing, but they would not reduce earnings when business was bad because the employee's average pay would fall along with decreasing sales. He feels that workers might be willing to take a pay cut in exchange for job security.

From this premise, Professor Weitzman reasons that if many or all companies installed the share system, the pool of qualified people looking for work would be quickly depleted, and we would have full employment. The increased purchasing power to take up all of this new productive capacity would come from the sizeable increase in employment and demand for goods and services.

While labor unions have expressed opposition to the Weitzman scheme because in the first instance it would reduce wages and increase the number of workers sharing the pie, Weitzman believes that this opposition could be overcome by having the government give income-tax breaks to those workers who accept the plan, in the form of capital gains treatments of part of their income or some such tax saving.

Professor Weitzman cites Japan as a successful example of the share system, for in many Japanese companies, as much as half of a worker's pay comes in the form of a bonus that is tied to the company's performance.

The New York Times called the Weitzman plan "Best Idea Since Keynes" in its lead editorial of March 28, 1985, repeating this support in an editorial of April 9, 1985, and an editorial discussion in its "Editorial Notebook" department of April 25, 1985. This *New York*

Times praise sparked some dissent from the economics community. In a letter to the editor of the *Times* on April 7, 1985, Rutgers University economics professor Paul Davidson, who is editor of the *Journal of Post-Keynesian Economics*, wrote:

> The "share economy" is merely an extension of the ancient agriculture system of agreeing to share sales revenues from future farm production known as sharecropping. History shows that the sharecropping system virtually disappeared from modern agriculture because it did not provide incentives for the capitalist-landowner to apply labor-saving, cost-efficient technology, while it simultaneously tended to reduce the real income of the wage-earning sharecropper to a bare subsistence. To reinstate a share-cropping scheme for the entire economy would merely reinstate these dreadful economic conditions.
>
> Mr. Weitzman's proposal would remove incentives for managers to minimize labor use by striving for increases in labor productivity and its operations. After entering into an industry-wide sharing contract, management would increase the rate of return to shareholders by replacing plant and equipment as it wore out with workers....Despite your claim that the share economy would resemble a full-employment economy, the share economy could not guarantee demand sufficient to generate full employment.

Weitzman's suggestion, although not adopted by business or labor groups immediately, has attracted widespread media and political interest, especially in the United Kingdom. The Liberal Party of Great Britain has taken up the idea, and Roger Carroll, a member of the City SDP's policy study group, commented favorably on it in the *City Periscope*, Spring 1985. Obviously, Professor Weitzman's challenging ideas deserve careful consideration and further development. But even if all his assumptions are correct, it seems to me that his profit-sharing scheme would require an additional source of income in order to be palatable to labor. In the first instance, it requires wage reductions and increases in the work force that would be very frightening to those who already hold well-paying jobs.

This point has been made by such highly qualified commentators as Dr. David Owen (in his 1985 Gaitskell Memorial Lecture, SDP *Open Forum* No. 9); Professor James E. Meade ("Wage-Fixing Revisited," The Institute of Economic Affairs Occasional Paper 72, 1985); and Samuel Brittan ("Economic Viewpoint," *Financial Times*, July 4, 1985; "Thatcherism & Beyond," *Encounter*, April 1985). These articles point up the formidable new conflicts of interest that would be created by replacing present wage systems with share systems reminiscent of earlier economic eras. Among the more troublesome conflicts are management's new incentive to forego capital investment in favor of a more profitable labor-intensive policy (as pointed out in Professor Paul Davidson's letter to the *Times*), and the resistance of present jobholders to cutting their own take-home pay in order to make jobs for outsiders. Without some very substantial counterweight to these negative forces, the Weitzman scheme would appear to be politically risky, since its implementation requires massive wage reductions that could easily be characterized as anti-labor. Dr. Owen, Professor Meade, and Mr. Brittan all recognize this, and they suggest such antidotes as tax relief and supplemental income from capital ownership.

In my opinion, the second income from capital ownership needed to make the Weitzman plan palatable would have to be rather substantial, beyond the tokenism of a few hundred pounds or a few hundred dollars per year. That is why I believe that USOP is the missing link to make the Weitzman plan—and any other plans for incentive pay linked to performance—palatable and viable. This is a fertile area for you essayists, a chance to build the bridge that American and British politicians and economists are groping for.

4d. Effects on Big Business, Stock Exchanges, Present Shareholders and the Rich

Since big business would be directly affected by USOP, what kind of response might we expect from the corporate sector? A few enlightened business leaders who are familiar with USOP realize it is probably our best hope of saving capitalism. Others, however, will need to be persuaded. Those who favor the plan are executives of large corporations whose share ownership is already widely diffused. They view USOP as a means of making capitalism work for everyone, but they also recognize the dangers of allowing USOP shares to be traded freely. The potential for exploitation by groups of political and social activists who know nothing about running a business is, in fact, the main reason I have suggested that USOP shares be nonvoting and nontransferable. These features should make the plan more attractive to business leaders who might otherwise worry about losing corporate control.

Such concerns apart, USOP does offer business leaders a very important benefit: the ability to raise the trillions of dollars industry will need for new plant and equipment over the rest of this century.

Under the present system, nobody really knows where this money will come from. The United States and Great Britain have already fallen way behind other industrial nations in the percentage of Gross Domestic Product (the yardstick used for international comparisons) devoted to fixed investment. In 1985, for example, our investment was 18.3 percent of GDP; Great Britain's was 19 percent; and Japan's was 30.8 percent. Reaganomics was supposed to spur capital investment, but it has had the opposite effect. Business leaders also worry about the extent of foreign stock ownership in our major corporations, including large blocks held by Arab nations.

Then there is the crying need for innovative research in private industry. Economic pressures have forced many businesses to hold the line with yesterday's products, instead of trying to replace them by expensive scientific breakthroughs. The number of patents granted to Americans fell very sharply during the 1970s, as did the number of innovative American products appearing on the market. As a consequence, we have been forced to import a lot of new technology from abroad. Only an affluent society will be able to fund the kind of research and development needed to increase productivity and economic growth.

A case in point: the need for new energy sources led to the government's Synfuel plan—taxing the oil companies' windfall profits and using that money for grants and government-sponsored research. Unfortunately, that research is not likely to yield positive results because the plan seems unpromising and has virtually been abandoned. Through USOP, however, the oil companies would have the necessary capital to research and develop new sources of energy. They would also have the support of the American public. After all, with everybody sharing the dividends, who is likely to complain about excessive profits? The friction between "big" oil and the "little" energy consumers would disappear, and with it, the need to impose an inefficient excess-profits tax. USOP, then, would enable us to fight the energy crisis via the real strengths of private enterprise, instead of struggling with the kind of government programs that have never really worked in the United States.

If this facilitation of capital funding were not incentive enough, USOP provides corporate executives with another important tool: a weapon in their fight against labor union interference. Some business leaders are aware of the ominous possibilities raised by Sweden's Meidner plan, which would open the way for labor union control of major corporations. They are also keeping a wary eye on the movement toward pension fund socialism here at home, which began with the AFL-CIO's 1980 decision to back "social investing" of such funds.

Another area in which USOP would help business is in overcoming the possibly negative effects of proposed income tax reform on business investment. The U.S. Treasury Department's 1985 proposals for reforming the Internal Revenue Code would eliminate the investment tax credit and reverse the 1981 liberalization of depreciation allowances. If such reforms are enacted, business may have a more difficult time raising the money needed for capital additions. But here USOP would create an entirely new source of funds for capital additions, which would not be inhibited or affected by tax reform.

A question you essayists might address: If big business does not support USOP, are they likely to have a more socialistic solution imposed upon them eventually, as has already happened in Great Britain and other western industrial democracies?

Clearly, USOP could be of great service to American business. But what about Wall Street—the bankers, brokers, and financiers who traditionally have played large roles in raising the $300 billion spent annually on new capital additions? At first blush, Wall Street (and its London counterpart, the City) might appear to be losers under USOP: their traditional financing services would not be needed to raise funds for capital expansion of our 2,000 leading corporations, nor could they expect to reap any direct benefit from USOP shares since they would not be traded publicly. But Wall Street and the City need not be shut out of the USOP process. I have no doubt that ingenious investment bankers would devise ways to take part in the underwriting and distribution of USOP shares. In any case, regular shares of stock would continue to be traded, as part of an expanded economy that is bound to be bullish for the investment community.

Indeed, under USOP, the supply of tradeable stocks and bonds would be diminished because USOP shares would be taking the place of securities that are now issued to pay for capital additions. This should increase demand for the stock that remains tradeable in relation to supply, and the value of the existing tradeable stock should therefore increase.

Restructuring through leveraged buyouts and "going private" have already reduced the number of shares publicly traded, and indeed have taken whole entities entirely out of the stock market. *Business Week* reported that in 1984, $78 billion of corporate equity vanished, while debt was increased by $169 billion. Yet, a major article in the *Wall Street Journal* of August 12, 1985 was headlined "Investment Banks See Gold Mine in Enthusiasm for Restructuring." What the investment bankers have lost in trading of public shares, they have more than recovered in their new roles in creative financial structuring to meet the reduction in publicly-traded securities. Some of you essayists may wish to address this question: How can the investment bankers of Wall Street and merchant bankers of the City play a useful role in the underwriting and distribution of USOP shares?

The resurgence of national unity and morale should also give the investment community a big lift, since it runs on emotional as well as statistical fuel. But the biggest boost—perhaps the largest single dose of good news in financial history—would be the elimination of the corporate income tax, an essential part of the USOP scheme. In the wake of such a move, we could expect a dramatic rise in corporate profits, and a lot more money flowing into the economy, all of which would stimulate growth and open the way for many new ventures. This would create lots of potential business for investment bankers and securities brokers, since the new ventures would not be eligible for USOP financing. Wall Street has always been proud of its role in creating new industries, and USOP would enhance that function.

Thus, USOP would not mean the end of the stock market. In fact, it could mean a new beginning—a real capital market based on performance and dividends rather than speculation and hype. And a chance for Wall Street and the City to lead the rebirth of capitalism by helping to create and finance many new businesses, instead of papering over old enterprises and destroying jobs in the process.

To summarize, I believe USOP would have a very positive effect on the stock markets. USOP shares would not be traded publicly, so they could not depress the regular share market. USOP would supply our economy's missing link: mass purchasing power to match our huge productive power. This should increase production and profits, and eventually raise share prices. It should also create a political climate in which everyone would be pulling for the major companies to increase profits, instead of the present tug-of-war that puts most of our citizens in an adversary position against business. A nation composed entirely of shareholder-capitalists would be a boon to Wall Street and the City. Once we installed USOP, the corporate income tax would become superfluous, which should boost corporate earnings to record high levels.

The present shareholders in our 2,000 leading corporations could argue, with at least technical justification, that the future value of their shares would be diminished under USOP. After all, they bought their shares when the corporate financing system was rigged to assure them ownership of capital the corporation would acquire in the future. This assurance was one of the things they paid for, and it was reflected in the price of their shares. They might also argue that they are being deprived of the benefits of the corporations' credit power.

Right now, as we've seen, debt—in the form of bonds and loans—pays for a substantial portion of new capital investments, which means that current shareholders increase the value of their stock without dipping into their own pockets. USOP, however, would put this credit power into new hands, using it to finance share ownership for the noncapitalists. For this reason, while USOP is based solely on *new* capital investments, it is not entirely accurate to say that this capital is not owned or claimed by anyone now; under the present system it would automatically be owned by current shareholders. So USOP might indeed put downward pressure on the value of outstanding stock, at least temporarily, even though the shares acquired by USOP shareholders would be issued at market value.

In his article, "Thatcherism and Beyond," (*Encounter* magazine, April 1985, page 60) British commentator Samuel Brittan mentions this dilution factor of USOP:

> No scheme for allocating share capital *gratis* to the have-nots can avoid "watering" the capital of existing shareholders. But Speiser's watering is of the gentlest. There is no confiscation; and mass shareownership relates to new capital, leaving ownership of existing assets unaffected.

If we're going to make capitalism work for everyone, something has to give. There is no free lunch, as traditional economists are so fond of saying. But any reduction in future share values should be more than offset by the overall benefits of USOP to the economy. Moreover, the present system is breaking down, and in the stagnating economy created by welfare capitalism, present shareholders are not likely to see the market value of their shares multiply as they did in years past. During the 1970s and 1980s, even with the old plumbing system in place, share values were eroded by billions of dollars. Thus, the present shareholders' position must be compared with their *real* future expectations under inflationary welfare capitalism—not with meaningless dreams of past glory. In fact, as long as we try to revive the economy via traditional methods, their position is likely to be worse than it would be under USOP. After all, what will their shares be worth if the government is forced to raise taxes to oppressively high levels, tap the pension funds, or print money indiscriminately in order to sustain the present system?

When stock is issued at market value for new capital acquisition, its value is not diluted. The 1985 Nobel Laureate in Economics, M.I.T. Professor Franco Modigliani, established in a famous 1958 paper that the value of a company's shares is not affected by the choice between issuing shares or using debt to raise money. When shares are used, each shareholder owns a slightly smaller percentage of the pie, but nobody loses, since the pie itself becomes larger and everything stays in proportion. In the case of USOP, there would be no dilution of political control, since USOP shares would be issued as nonvoting stock.

Today's regular shareholders must realize that the growth factor of capital additions is largely an illusion in an economy that is as shaky as the present welfare-capitalist system. If share prices had actually kept pace with inflation, the Dow-Jones industrial average would be over 5,000, whereas it has barely cleared the 1,400 mark. The phasing out of the corporate income tax, and the revitalization of the entire economy which most likely would accompany USOP, should benefit every shareholder, old or new, through increased production, profits, and financial stability. Thus, we need not fret about the position of the present shareholders.

If you're troubled by the concept of using the credit power of our major corporations to benefit 50 million noncapitalist households (as USOP would), then consider the latest free market maneuver that uses this credit power to benefit a mere handful of people—the leveraged buyout. Formerly known by the more descriptive term of "bootstrap financing," the typical leveraged buyout will involve a few top executives of a large corporation who want to take over ownership for themselves, using the assets of the corporation as collateral for huge loans with which to buy out the present stockholders. Leveraged buyouts do not create jobs, raise profits, increase production, or improve management. Yet, our major lenders have made billions of dollars available for such bootstrap financing, and nobody questions the legitimacy of using the assets of major corporations to create hundreds of millions in profits out of mere paper transactions. Indeed, a recent advertisement by the First Boston Corporation, a leading investment banker in leveraged buyouts, proclaims that First Boston is adept at "devising complex structures to provide managements with substantial and preferential equity positions in the new buy-out company" (*National Law Journal*, August 19, 1985, p. 19).

Although most Americans do not now benefit from capital ownership, to a great extent they are already footing the bill for new capital, in the form of the huge government subsidies and tax breaks offered to big business. Today, a good chunk of the financing needed for new capital comes directly from the government—funded, of course, with taxpayers' dollars. There is, for example, the investment tax credit, which amounts to an outright gift from the taxpayers to our businesses.

Then there are depreciation allowances, credits for adding new employees, and numerous other tax advantages which we have purposely allowed to businesses to keep them healthy. These tax breaks also help the present stockholders to own new capital without investing any more money.

When it comes to building new plants, there are even more direct government subsidies. When executives of our giant corporations announce a decision to build a new plant, their first move is to shop for government grants and tax breaks. From the federal government they would seek, and probably get, huge grants from the Department of Housing and Urban Development for the acquisition of land and relocation of residents. Such grants may exceed $100 million for a single new plant. The corporation will also shop for state and local grants, subsidies, and tax breaks, so that in the end a large portion of the cost of new plants is borne by the taxpayers.

Once the plant is built, the sale of the products produced in the plant is often financed or subsidized by the government. For example, the large portion of our aircraft output that is sold overseas is financed by low-interest loans granted by the Export-Import Bank in Washington. Without that government aid, our aircraft manufacturers could not compete in the world markets. But this assistance doesn't come cheaply. In opposing the 1984 budget cuts in social welfare programs, Public Citizens' Congress Watch pointed out that five major "corporate welfare" items (the Synthetic Fuels Corporation, the investment tax credit, accelerated depreciation, the Export-Import Bank, and oil industry tax breaks) cost American taxpayers $65 billion a year. And in 1984, American businesses benefited from the issuance of more than $71 billion worth of industrial development bonds, another federally-subsidized, low-interest loan program that provides financing for new business projects through tax-exempt bonds.

Indeed, the taxpayers provide American business with many billions of dollars' worth of facilities for which the businesses pay little or nothing by way of capital investments, such as roads, bridges, harbors, and airports. So if anyone tells you USOP will interfere with private enterprise, or that low-interest government-guaranteed loans will disrupt our banking system, don't believe them. Our major corporations don't take the kind of entrepreneurial risks they did 50 years ago. Their capital additions are substantially subsidized by the public treasury. Since the public is already paying much of the bill, why should all that new capital automatically be owned by the present shareholders?

This trick of retaining full ownership of capital paid for by the government has not endeared big business to most Americans. In 1965, the Opinion Research Company surveyed Americans' attitudes about business, asking whether the corporate sector was making too much profit, a reasonable profit, or not enough profit. Fourteen percent of the people polled at that time believed corporate profits were excessive. By 1979, however, that figure had swelled to 51 percent. Clearly, the average noncapitalist does not look kindly on business profits, even though profits have actually been shrinking and have virtually disappeared in major industries like coal, steel, and housing. Yet if all Americans were receiving dividends, it would probably be hard to find anyone willing to complain that business was reaping excessive profit. Nor would we see the kind of political tug-of-war that now puts most of our citizens in an adversarial position against the major companies. Today most Americans want big business to achieve the impossible: more jobs, higher wages, higher corporate taxes, higher pension contributions, lower prices, and better products. Under USOP, these pressures would be eased, and for the first time it would be politically feasible to eliminate the corporate income tax. That would benefit present shareholders enormously, and would more than compensate for any imagined dilution in the value of their shares.

Like the present shareholders in our major corporations, the very rich probably wouldn't welcome USOP with much enthusiasm. But, in fact, USOP would offer them protection against the possibility of confiscation through a wealth tax or even more drastic measures. As long as welfare capitalism fails to provide an adequate income for most citizens, capitalism itself is in danger. As Senator Russell B. Long has pointed out in many speeches, people who are already wealthy will be much more secure in their wealth when capitalism becomes a good deal for everyone. Otherwise, as tax expert Long puts it, "They're going to wind up at a minimum having their eyeballs taxed off them." Beyond that minimum is the risk that the failings of welfare capitalism will lead to socialism, as has already happened in Great Britain and in many other Western democracies. Instead, via USOP, the rich could finally utter the word "capitalist" without whispering. Receiving income from MOP ownership would become acceptable behavior in a capitalist society, if everyone got the chance to become a capitalist.

So much for my arguments. This is an important area in which to do your own thinking, because we need the support of business, shareholders, and investment bankers, and it will take more than my opinion to convince them that USOP is in their best interests. I have outlined the case for USOP's favorable effects on business and on stock prices through elimination of the corporate income tax, higher dividend payments, addition of new purchasing power, creation of a probusiness climate, reduction of the supply of tradeable securities, and reduction of corporate interest expenses. But some analysts believe that USOP will depress stock prices because it will deprive present shareholders of future earnings arising from expansion. They argue that the growth factor will largely benefit the USOP shareholders, through their ownership of the right to receive income from all the new plants and equipment. Professor Lawrence R. Klein addressed this question in his comments at the 1977 Brookings Institution seminar (see Appendix A). He concluded:

> In many cases, it may be expected that the additional investment made possible by the acquisition of Plan funds by business will increase the productivity of existing capital or capital acquired contemporaneously outside the Plan. As investment is enhanced throughout the whole economy, firms generally will benefit from the induced increase in total output.

Some economists believe that the ability of management to invest, leverage, and otherwise deploy retained earnings is an important factor in stock prices, and that this ability is largely nullified by USOP's requirement that retained earnings be paid out as dividends. Some also have the same feeling about management's ability to use the leverage of debt. Notwithstanding Professor Klein's optimism and my laundry list of USOP's benefits to business, these are serious arguments that require detailed answers. Would business be better off without the expense of debt? Would the increased dividends resulting from the payout of retained earnings compensate for loss of management's ability to deploy these earnings in other ways? If not, can you suggest modifications of the Kitty Hawk model to compensate for these factors? For example, should management be allowed to use part or all of retained earnings under certain circumstances? Likewise, as to debt?

4e. Effects on Specific Groups: Women, Minorities, Youth, etc.

Following are some general observations on the potential effects of the Kitty Hawk model of USOP on various groups of people. These observations deal mainly with the American scene, but unless otherwise indicated, they are applicable to Great Britain as well.

Women: Despite recent legislation, equal treatment in hiring, salary, and promotion remain largely in the hands of top management, which is still very much a man's world. So very few women have the chance to become entrepreneurs or shareholders, except through inheritance. Share ownership, however, would give women real economic independence for the first time, and what better way to achieve such ownership than through a plan that would distribute it to all households without regard to gender.

Blacks and other ethnic minorities: For more than 20 years, the American government has tried to bring blacks and other minority groups into the mainstream of society via training and affirmative action programs. Unfortunately, their efforts have proved largely unsuccessful. Some black leaders believe these programs simply perpetuate the welfare mentality. And many blacks who get jobs through these programs feel they are being forced to work in a white man's world under a white man's rules, in an environment that's not likely to give them a fair shake no matter how hard they work. This attitude often affects their performance, so they remain at the bottom of the economic ladder, all of which feeds their belief that they would be better off on welfare.

Doubts about the value of government programs are not limited to working-class blacks. In recent years, black intellectuals have begun to oppose programs like busing and affirmative action because they stir up a lot of resentment among whites without providing many real benefits for blacks. And the old liberal faith in education as a cure-all for social problems is fading. Indeed, the unemployment rate among blacks today is higher than it was in the 1960s when education, training, and affirmative action programs were launched. The problem is that anti-inflation policies hit the blacks first because they result in layoffs that start at the lowest economic level. While this is not usually a result of racial prejudice, it certainly has the same effect.

Are jobs the answer? Our politicians still seem to think so, but none can deliver on their campaign promises of employment because the system itself can no longer create enough jobs—for blacks or whites. Entrepreneurship is not the answer either. Venture capital and starting up new businesses are games for the rich, who can afford to take losses on most of their investments and make them up on the one out of ten that hits the jackpot. What blacks really need is a piece of the action—shares in existing successful enterprises, which are now almost entirely owned by white people. USOP would, therefore, bring blacks and other ethnic minorities into the mainstream of capitalism and make them full participants in American life for the first time.

Youth: It's difficult to generalize about any group that runs the gamut from committed careerists to revolutionary activists to dropouts. But with our youth, we seem to have moved beyond the self-indulgent "me" generation, and most young people are looking for a new idea, something they can take hold of and use to build a new American dream. But what do they have to work with? Middle class youths face downward mobility for the first time in our history, and under our present system, they are not likely to equal their parents' standard of living. So it's not surprising that they are loath to bring children into such a world and see little point in saving for a brighter future. They just don't believe a brighter future will arrive. Nor is their cynicism unwarranted; time and again they've heard politicians promise to make America great again, without having the semblance of a plan that can do so.

Some would argue that the prospect of reduced middle class wealth is a natural consequence of the twentieth century egalitarian leveling process. As the poor use the ballot box to achieve economic gains, somebody has to pay. And the very rich are too few in number and too well fortified in their tax shelters to foot the huge bill presented in the name of social justice. But whether this process is natural or not, it's certainly not healthy for the future of capitalism. As more of the nonvoting half of our population becomes voters, socialism is likely to win eventually at the polls.

Our youth has more to lose from the end of the American dream than anyone else. They seem very cynical. But if you sit down with college students and explain USOP to them for five minutes, you can see their eyes light up. They are literally hungering after a plan that will give them a brigher future. They've tried everything—drugs, narcissism, religious cults—and they know these are not the solutions. But a plan with the scope and daring of USOP is made to order for our youth.

The alienation of British youth is even more pronounced, since millions of teenagers face the prospect of little or no permanent employment in the foreseeable future. This may be one of the causes of hooliganism and soccer riots. In any case, it is a pitiful waste of a generation of people who are ready, willing, and able to build better lives for themselves and to improve their nation.

Senior citizens and retired workers: Because it will take at least seven years for the USOP shares to pay for themselves, seniors and retired workers have less to gain from its adoption; many will not reap direct benefits of USOP share ownership in their lifetimes. However, their financial security is constantly threatened by the potential insolvency of the Social Security system. USOP would remove this threat by gradually assuming the financial burden now carried by Social Security. At the very least, senior citizens would no longer be considered millstones around the necks of the young and working people. Moreover, they would benefit directly from the strengthening of the economy, and could appreciate the greatly enhanced prospects facing their children and grandchildren under USOP.

Consumers: Consumer activists have special reasons for supporting USOP. With millions of individuals owning capital, they would gain economic power impossible to muster through any consumer organization. This power would represent a strong safeguard against the excesses of big business, big labor, and big government—the three superpowers against whom consumer activists usually fight a losing battle.

But if all citizens become capitalists, wouldn't they root for unlimited corporate profits, which in turn would affect consumers adversely? I don't believe so. A rejuvenated economy would foster plenty of competition, with "the lowest price for the best quality" still determining what consumers will buy. And as the economy booms, many new products would appear on the market. There is no basis for assuming that consumers who are also shareholders of our major companies would allow prices to rise unreasonably; if price inflation ate up the benefits, their newly gained dividends would not improve their finances.

The labor unions: It is quite likely that labor leaders would initially shun USOP, preferring instead to work for pension fund socialism and Meidner-type plans, which give unions stock control of major businesses. However, the workers themselves would be much better off under USOP; not only would they own shares outright, but they would also receive dividend income well before retirement age.

Traditionally, American labor leaders have shied away from worker ownership, fearing that if workers became shareholders, they would be less interested in union representation. Early union leaders even opposed pension plans when they first came on the scene. These fears may be valid when employees own shares in the companies for which they work, because their loyalties are split between labor and management. They may want higher wages, but not if that would mean lower profits. But with USOP, workers get a share of American or British industry rather than shares in their own companies, so there is no reason to believe they would be less interested in having the unions negotiate their wage demands. However, those demands might be less militant since workers would also receive the wages of capital and would have a vested interest in the success of big business.

USOP should be attractive to Britain's Labour Party because unlike employee ownership, it does not drive a wedge between the worker and the trade union.

Farmers: USOP would be a bonanza for our farmers. For the first time, they would not be entirely dependent on the vagaries of weather and crop yields for their income. And by making agriculture a capital-owning partner in industry, the long-running friction between these segments of our society would dissipate. Such a move might even serve to reduce our enormous expenditures for agricultural subsidies.

Professionals: USOP represents an important opportunity for economists, lawyers, accountants, educators, and intellectuals, whose special skills equip them to shape the plan. Rather than continuing to squander their talents on tax shelters and welfare schemes, they can serve the nation by educating the public on USOP and helping to develop a detailed plan for its implementation.

Lawyers and accountants helped to make the stock corporation an efficient tool of capitalism. But now the corporation is in danger of obsolescence, because the lawyer-designed corporate finance system perpetuates the overconcentration of capital ownership and doesn't distribute purchasing power equitably enough. We need the expertise of a lot more lawyers to perfect USOP, and since the concept of justice is the central thrust of USOP, this might make lawyers popular for a change.

On a more personal level, USOP serves the interests of our professional class. They are, after all, among the economic elite who have the most to lose if capitalism doesn't survive.

Environmentalists and ecologists: The first reaction of an environmentalist to the USOP concept is usually negative, a feeling that the plan would be a disaster for our environment because all Americans and Britons would become committed to the success of our major corporations, and there would be nobody left to oppose the exploitation of our natural resources for corporate profit. But concern about pollution is often put aside when we run into inflation, unemployment, and capital shortages under welfare capitalism.

Consider the town with the bucolic name of Naturita, Colorado, which made the news in July of 1982 by announcing that it had won a $10 million industrial project that would create 100 new jobs for the 900 people who live in Naturita. What was the project so eagerly pursued? Operation of a nuclear waste dump! And why were they so willing to turn their town into an ecological disaster area? Because they had been battling economic depression since the early 1980s, when the uranium industry on which they depended went into a major slump.

Only a truly affluent society can afford to protect the environment against the ravages of industry. Right now, the funds needed for environmental protection are being channeled into the arms race and our futile struggle to maintain economic growth through wages and welfare. The environmentalists need USOP as badly as anyone else; they should climb aboard and start the process of shaping USOP so it becomes a force for cleaning up pollution rather than increasing it. We must find new methods and new fuels to keep our standard of living high and yet keep our environment safe. This will require huge amounts of new capital that neither government nor private industry can muster without a fundamental policy change like USOP.

Small businesses: USOP could represent a potential threat to small business, since it favors large businesses by making huge sums available to them for new capital expenditures. Eventually, we should be able to include smaller companies in the USOP system, but we will have to begin with our 2,000 largest successful companies because we are trying to plug our neediest people into the strongest sector of our economy. (See Section 3f for discussion of broadening USOP to encompass interests in smaller businesses.)

Of course, traditional sources of capital would remain available to smaller businesses. In fact, financiers and bankers would take more interest in them because the larger corporations would no longer constitute a captive market. This would motivate investment bankers to concentrate on one of their most important functions: helping to develop new businesses, new products, and new jobs through venture capital and other creative methods of financing.

I don't think USOP would make the situation any worse for small business than it already is under welfare capitalism, which does little to promote the survival and prosperity of small businesses. Government venture capital programs—giving the small entrepreneur a few hundred thousand dollars to compete with the giants—usually are dismal failures. The government also tries to subsidize small businesses with low-interest loans, free management assistance, and by restricting some procurement contracts to bids from small companies. However, these programs don't have a significant impact on our economy, and most small business proprietors are forced to live by their wits.

While the 2,000 large companies participating in USOP at the outset would gain some advantages, they would not be insulated from the effects of bad business decisions. They would have to justify outlays for capital additions just as before, demonstrating to their directors, shareholders, and bankers that the new capital would pay for itself out of its own earnings. These companies would lose just as much from unsuccessful projects as under the present system. If Peerless Pizza's new plant turns out to be a $10 million lemon, Peerless will lose the $10 million it invested in the plant, for which it issued that amount of stock to the USOP fund. While the federal government would guarantee payment of the $10 million loans by banks to pay for the Peerless shares distributed to USOP shareholders, the government guarantee would have nothing to do with Peerless itself or the plant that Peerless built.

4f. Religious Aspects

While many religious leaders have increased their efforts to explore the moral dimensions of economic decisions and to advocate concrete steps toward achieving social justice, the shortcomings of the two apparent choices—welfare capitalism and democratic socialism—have confronted religous leaders with the dilemma of having to choose between two defective systems. Therefore, it would appear that a new approach which combines some of the best features of capitalism and socialism in order to achieve social justice, would be attractive to religious leaders who, in turn, are in a position to influence millions of potential supporters of USOP.

The widespread favorable comment from important figures in the mainline Protestant churches on the work of the National Conference of Catholic Bishops in their drafting of a pastoral letter on "Catholic Social Teaching and the U. S. Economy," shows the concern among both Protestant and Catholic churches. This courageous attempt to state the problems of the American economy and to apply moral standards in seeking remedies, has caused much controversy. The latest draft of the pastoral, published October 7, 1985, contains these recommendations:

> 288. Workers in firms and on farms are especially in need of stronger institutional protection, for their jobs and livelihood are particularly vulnerable to the decisions of others in today's highly competitive labor market. Several new arrangements are gaining new support in the United States: profit sharing by the workers in a firm; enabling employees to become company stockholders; granting employees greater participation in determining the conditions of work; cooperative ownership of the firm by all who work within it; and *schemes for enabling a much larger number of Americans, regardless of their employment status, to become shareholders in successful corporations*. Initiatives of this

sort can enhance productivity, increase the profitability of firms,
provide greater job security and work satisfaction for employees,
and reduce adversarial relations.)
    289. None of these approaches provides a panacea, and all
have certain drawbacks. Nevertheless we believe that continued
research and experimentation with these approaches will be of
benefit....(Italics supplied)

The italicized portion of No. 288 shows that USOP has important
religious and moral implications, for USOP is the only one of the
arrangements mentioned in that paragraph that would substantially
benefit the people to whom the pastoral is dedicated: the poor. Protestant organizations such as the National Council of Churches of Christ
in America and the World Council of Churches (based in Geneva,
Switzerland) would also find in USOP a potential prize in their search
for an economic approach that is not exploitative and yet maintains
the productive energy of capitalism, sharing its benefits with the entire
populace.

    Could USOP help to solve the crushing economic and social
problems of Latin America? One can well sympathize with the Latin
American clergy who are called upon to bury babies and others who
suffer from malnutrition and other effects of poverty. But wouldn't
their task be eased if they did not have to choose between the brand
of capitalism that exploits their impoverished people while the rich
smuggle huge sums of money to numbered Swiss bank accounts—and
Marxism, which usually brings little in the way of freedom or economic
advancement for the masses? What if the Latin American clergy had
a third choice: a system that preserves the private initiative and productivity of capitalism and the humane concern of socialist theory?

    The British clergymen with whom I have discussed this question
are equally dedicated to social justice and are as much in need of a
fresh solution as the American clergy. But many clergymen in the
United Kingdom, as in the United States, laboring under the assumption
that capitalism must be exploitative, have decided that they cannot
lead the way to social justice without first taking the step of replacing
capitalism with some form of Marxism.

    Here are some questions that you might address in your essay:

    What are the religious implications of USOP?

    Could USOP make capitalism a more moral, ethical system that
would come closer to the religious ideal of social justice?

    Could USOP solve any of the problems raised in the American
Catholic Bishops' pastoral letter?

    How can religious organizations promote discussion of USOP?

5.

ECONOMIC FEASIBILITY OF USOP

Please note that there is some overlap between the discussions of economic feasibility in this section and political feasibility in the following section. It is difficult to separate these two forms of feasibility. As we have seen, most economists believe that income distribution is a political question, and that the legislature is free to distribute income through capital ownership rather than through transfer payments or a welfare system if it so chooses. Accordingly, since USOP is basically a change in income distribution, using capital ownership rather than transfer payments as the mechanism, the science of economics is neutral on this point, and there is no theoretical economic barrier to implementation of USOP.

All the good intentions in the world will not help if USOP is not an economically feasible idea. It should comfort you to learn that the basic concept behind USOP has been scrutinized by such authorities as the Joint Economic Committee of Congress; a full-day seminar held at the Brookings Institution in 1977; and a symposium arranged by the *Journal of Post-Keynesian Economics* in 1985. None of these examinations revealed any technical or theoretical flaws in the concept. Indeed, they produced authoritative support for the economic feasibility of USOP. Nevertheless, you are free to examine the question *de novo* and come up with your own answer to the economic feasibility question.

Because it is all too easy to question the feasibility of any proposal for structural change in the economic system, we should start out with a broad overview. A sound one is provided by Princeton University Professor Alan S. Blinder in his essay, "Economic Policy Can be Hard-Headed—and Soft-Hearted," published in *Business Week*, August 12, 1985. Professor Blinder deals with two underlying principles of the economy: the Principle of Efficiency, which demands that economic policies make our economic system more productive; and the Principle of Equity, which holds that assisting society's underdogs is a proper function of government. His essay suggests that any policy change that is contrary to both the Principle of Efficiency and the Principle of Equity should be rejected; that policies which comport with one or the other principle should be considered; and that if the proposed policy promotes both efficiency and equity, it probably merits adoption. This should help to guide your own formulation of policies to make USOP economically feasible.

Now, back to the historical evidence of USOP's feasibility. In 1976, I brought to the attention of the Joint Economic Committee of Congress (JEC) a plan that was similar in concept to the Kitty Hawk model of USOP. At the time, the JEC was conducting hearings on Employee Stock Ownership Plans (ESOPs) and other similar programs, and I suggested that the inquiry be broadened to include plans which were not based on the employment relationship. The JEC, which is our government's main forum for new economic ideas, found the concept promising, and unanimously approved these recommendations in its 1976 Joint Economic Report:

> To begin to diffuse the ownership of capital and to provide an opportunity for citizens of moderate income to become owners of capital rather than relying solely on their labor as a source of income and security, the Committee recommends the adoption of a national policy to foster the goal of broadened ownership. The spirit of this goal and what it purports to accomplish was endorsed by many of the witnesses at our regional hearings. [p. 99]

Although the JEC did not recommend any specific method of providing capital ownership to citizens at large, it concluded:

> Whatever the means used, a basic objective should be to distribute *newly created capital* broadly among the population. Such a policy would redress a major imbalance in our society and has the potential for strengthening future business growth.
>
> To provide a realistic opportunity for more U.S. citizens to become owners of capital, and to provide an expanded source of

equity financing for corporations, it should be made national policy to pursue the goal of broadened capital ownership. Congress also should request from the Administration a quadrennial report on the ownership of wealth in this country which would assist in evaluating how successfully the base of wealth was being broadened over time. [Italics mine; pp. 99-100]

I was particularly gratified that the JEC used the words "distribute newly created capital broadly among the population," since it was the first government recognition of USOP's essence: the use of *new* capital to distribute income where it was needed most, rather than through employment channels. (The historical background of the plan, and the ways in which I modified it in conjunction with the JEC staff, are covered in my 1977 book, *A Piece of The Action.*)

In 1977, the concept was discussed at the Brookings Institution in an all-day seminar attended by about 35 economists, financial experts, and government officials. Numerous questions were raised, but most of those present agreed that the plan was worth a test, and no one pointed out any reason why it could not be made to work. A summary of the seminar will be found in Appendix A.

The Spring 1985 edition of the *Journal of Post-Keynesian Economics* (Vol. 7, No. 3) contained a symposium on broadening capital ownership, with papers by the *Journal*'s editor, Professor Paul Davidson; Professor Robert Lekachman, Distinguished Professor of Economics at Herbert Lehman College, City University of New York; Ward Morehouse, president of the Council on International and Public Affairs; and myself. These papers, which constitute the first analysis in depth of the USOP principle in a professional economics journal, are reproduced in Appendix B. (Please note that when these papers were written, the Kitty Hawk model of USOP was known as "SuperStock," and is so referred to by the authors in Appendix B.)

Professor Davidson points out some of the historical foundations for USOP, in the writings of John Maynard Keynes and Joan Robinson. Professor Lekachman considers USOP to "be a conservative alternative to the welfare state." He calls the notion of the Kitty Hawk model ingenious, and goes on to say that it "is feasible and it is very carefully worked out."

In Britain, the principal academic commentator on the feasibility of (and the need for) mass capital ownership is the Nobel Laureate James E. Meade, Professor Emeritus of Economics at Cambridge University. His 1964 book, *Efficiency, Equality, and the Ownership of Property* is a treasure chest of ideas for solving the economic prob-

lems of industrial democracies, particularly Chapter 5, "A Property-
Owning Democracy." More recently, Professor Meade has become
even more specific on the feasibility of capital ownership for all Brit-
ons. In his paper, "Full Employment, New Technologies and the
Distribution of Income," published in the *Journal of Social Policy*,
Vol 13, Part 2, April 1984, Professor Meade says:

> Surely there must be a better way of organizing our institutions
> so that new technologies which could enable everyone to have a
> higher standard of living than before will not threaten to lead to
> either of these disastrous situations. My answer would be to at-
> tempt to devise wage-setting institutions which would allow the
> real wage rate to fall to the extent necessary to provide employ-
> ment opportunities to all who sought them, but to combine this
> with fiscal and other institutions which ensured that directly or
> indirectly everyone enjoyed a fair share of the profits earned on
> the robots, computers, and tapes, and indeed on property in gen-
> eral....If every citizen were a representative owner of property
> as well as a representative earner of wages, the fact that an efficient
> use of the price mechanism required a fall in the wage rate relative
> to the return on the property would not affect the distribution of
> income as between individuals; everyone's property income would
> go up as their wage income went down. [pp. 139, 144]

Samuel Brittan, economics commentator and assistant editor of
the *Financial Times*, has written extensively on this subject. In 1984,
the *Financial Times* published a collection of his articles and papers,
entitled *Jobs, Pay, Unions and the Ownership of Capital*. In the preface
to that collection of articles, Mr. Brittan writes:

> The theme of these articles is that the demand for labour, as of
> anything else, is sensitive to its price, i.e. the level of real wages.
> Of course, there are many other forces which affect unemploy-
> ment. But we are unlikely to reverse the long-term upward drift
> in unemployment from one business cycle to the next, until pay
> levels, both in general and in particular occupations, and areas,
> move nearer to market-clearing levels.
> If, however, the rewards of capital are going to rise and those of
> labour to fall (whether absolutely or relatively), the question of
> "Who owns the capital?" becomes vital. Hence the urgency of
> my interest in a widespread distribution of equity ownership in
> which citizens who would not normally go near the Stock Ex-
> change are handed over a stake in the nation's capital assets.

In his 1983 book, *The Role and Limits of Government: Essays in Political Economy*, Mr. Brittan writes:

> Secondly, and ultimately more important, there will need to be a big shift in the ownership of productive property. The mistake of socialists and collectivists is that they attack the existence or size of profits rather than the ownership of profitable assets. If most wage earners were also capitalists, the social arguments against a shift to profits would disappear. This is partly happening through the pension funds, but adding further power to these funds has well-known drawbacks. A reform of Capital Transfer Tax to make it into an inheritance or accession tax, levied on the *recipient*, would be an encouragement to the dispersion of hereditary property.
>
> But more direct measures to give ordinary citizens a stake in the ownership of productive assets are also required. Workers' co-ops have certainly a role here, but I can see no case for making these the sole form of business enterprise and I can see disadvantages in workers having all their eggs—their equity property as well as their wage—in one basket. A good deal could be done by the "giving away" (at a sacrifice in Treasury revenue) of state-owned industries on the lines of a scheme by Barry Riley and myself for "A People's Stake in North Sea Oil" in which state revenue would be paid out directly to citizens, whose entitlements could be sold on the market. Going beyond that there is a case for public unit trusts, whose shares would be distributed to all citizens, to whom a growing proportion of the equity of each major company would be transferred. [pp. 260-261]

It seems clear, therefore, that USOP is (at least theoretically) feasible. The question remains, can we build a model that really works, and can we acquire the skills needed to make such a structural change successfully? In the words of the noted automobile designer, Enzo Ferrari, "What can be conceived can be created." In the United States and Great Britain, we already have the main ingredients needed to make USOP work: the most sophisticated credit and stock-corporation systems in the world. Moreover, since USOP is a more logical system than welfare capitalism and is more consistent with our national goals, it should be easier to manage than the present system.

At some point, the question will arise, "How does USOP differ from Senator George McGovern's 1972 campaign proposal of a $1,000 Treasury handout to every person who needs it?" Try your hand at formulating an answer. My brief answer is that McGovern's proposal would have produced socialist income—taking money from wage-earners through taxation and transferring it to needy individuals. USOP is based upon capitalist income—giving every citizen the chance to share in the profits of our leading companies. It ties everyone into the capitalist system, so that the welfare benefits as well as the dividends are paid from what all of us, working together, make the system earn. McGovern's plan would have distributed money produced by government deficits; USOP would distribute money produced by corporate profits. Some people feel this is merely a cosmetic difference. I believe it is a substantive difference. What do you think?

6.

POLITICAL FEASIBILITY OF USOP

It would be difficult to imagine a policy more suitable than USOP for creating national unity and improving morale. USOP is consistent with Anglo-American tradition, both liberal and conservative. It is conservative in that it would reduce taxes, eventually eliminate transfer payments, and check the growth of government bureaucracy, while preserving private ownership and existing financial institutions, and supporting business. It is liberal because it would do more for the ordinary individual than all of the government welfare schemes ever dreamed up. And it would enable Americans and Britons to achieve economic independence without relying on welfare.

As a new national economic policy, USOP would require extensive legislation and therefore broad political backing. But because it meets important objectives of the left, the right, and the center, it should receive over-whelming support from all sectors. And because it addresses everyone's concerns, it is the only solution capable of uniting us emotionally. In fact, like Marxism, USOP appeals to our most basic emotion—hope for a better future. Unlike Marxism, USOP can deliver on its promises without destroying democracy. It would put all of us on the same side and in the same class.

For the first time, our economic system would mirror our system of political democracy, and we would be affluent enough to deal with problems like poverty, pollution, health care, and crime. We would no longer have to feel guilty about an undemocratic, inequitable capitalist system, so we could begin to enforce the criminal law in good conscience.

One of the clearest indications that USOP is politically feasible is found in the 1976 Joint Economic Committee report, quoted in the preceding section. The JEC voted unanimously that it should be national policy to distribute newly created capital broadly among the population. The annual Joint Economic Report, mandated by the Employment Act of 1946, is a battleground of conflicting and diverging economic policy recommendations, which usually split very sharply along party lines. In the 1976 report, as in the others, there were many dissenting and discordant views expressed on numerous economic policy choices—but on the recommendation that broadened ownership of new capital should be new policy, there was complete unanimity.

In *The American Ethos: Public Attitudes Toward Capitalism and Democracy* by Herbert McClosky and John Zaller, the authors conclude:

> Our argument, then, can be summarized as follows: conflicts between capitalism and democracy remain a recurrent feature of American life; when these conflicts surface, they are likely to be resolved in ways predominantly favorable to the democractic tradition; and some type of welfare capitalism is the institutional form this resolution is likely to take. [p. 302]

But by 1985, most Americans were disillusioned with the costs and ineffectiveness of welfare capitalism, and were ready for a new idea. As pointed out by Professor Robert Lekachman in the *Journal of Post-Keynesian Economics* (see Appendix B), USOP is "a conservative alternative to the welfare state." Professor Lekachman goes on to say:

> We are a highly conservative, capitalist society. In fact, if I were engaged in marketing the [USOP] concept, I would present it as a basically conservative notion. If the Reagan administration is open to any new ideas in its second term, there would be a distinct possibility that the administration would perceive this idea as consistent with the ethos of ownership which runs through the official family.

Thus, conservatives could be very comfortable with the idea of officially adopting capitalism as part of the American way of life, by opening it to all citizens in a meaningful way: access to capital ownership.

For liberals and middle-of-the-road people, USOP offers an alternative to the broken dream of full employment. Obviously, full employment is the ideal solution to the problems of industrial capitalism; but just as clearly, capitalist nations are running out of the ability to provide enough well-paying jobs to justify the inequities of wealth ownership and income distribution. As early as 1936, John Maynard Keynes foresaw that modern industrial capitalism would not be able to sustain anything close to full employment and that capital ownership would have to take up the slack. In his masterwork, *The General Theory of Employment, Interest and Money*, Keynes wrote:

> The outstanding faults of the economic society in which we live are its failure to provide for full employment and its arbitrary and inequitable distribution of wealth and incomes....I conceive, therefore, that a somewhat comprehensive socialisation of investment will prove the only means of securing an approximation to full employment; though this need not exclude all manner of compromises and of devices by which public authority will co-operate with private initiative. But beyond this no obvious case is made out for a system of State Socialism which would embrace most of the economic life of the community. It is not the ownership of the instruments of production which it is important for the State to assume. If the State is able to determine the aggregate amount of resources devoted to augmenting the instruments and the basic rate of reward to those who own them, it will have accomplished all that is necessary. [pp. 372-78]

Thus, Keynes recognized that the Western democracies would need some form of socialization of capital ownership other than state socialism—one that would retain the individualism he saw as "the best safeguard of personal liberty." He also predicted that this socialization would be more favorable to world peace than the old system had been (p. 381).

When Great Britain entered World War II, Keynes perceived the buildup of inflationary pressures and decided that the way to check them was to give workers a share of capital profits. In his 1940 essay, "How to Pay for the War," he proposed a radical plan of forced savings to bring about the broadening of capital ownership. It was based on conditions of wartime Britain, and it had limited purposes, but it contained the following prophetic language:

> We cannot reward the worker [by raising wages] and an attempt to do so would merely set in motion the inflationary process. But we can reward him by giving him a share in claims on the future which would belong otherwise to the entrepreneurs.

Thus, at a time when income distribution through wages alone was threatening to cause inflation, Keynes's mind flashed to a new solution: income distribution through worker ownership of capital, or as he called it, "the accumulation of working-class wealth under working-class control." In the same essay, Keynes said this plan would bring "an advance toward economic equality greater than any which we have made in recent times."

Shortly before his death, Senator Hubert H. Humphrey of Minnesota declared:

> Throughout my career as a public servant, I have viewed full employment as a top priority goal for this country. And I continue to do so. But I recognize that capital, and the question of who owns it and therefore reaps the benefit of its productiveness, is an extremely important issue that is complementary to the issue of full employment.
>
> I see these as twin pillars of our economy: Full employment of our labor resources and widespread ownership of our capital resources. Such twin pillars would go a long way in providing a firm underlying support for future economic growth that would be equitably shared. [Congressional Record, Vol. 128, No. 7, February 3, 1982, p. S334]

Thus two great leaders of the recent past who were committed to the principle of full employment found that its economic and political equivalent could be achieved only through the broadening of capital ownership. What has been missing up to now is a specific plan that Keynes and Humphrey, as well as the political majority in their countries, could support.

In the United Kingdom, there has also been long-term, across-the-board support for the concept of broad capital ownership. The Wider Share Ownership Council, organized in 1959, from the outset has received support from all political sectors. Among the leading organizers of the WSOC were Toby Low (now Lord Aldington) and Maurice Macmillan of the Conservative Party, and Lord Harold Lever of the Labour Party. More recently, Dr. David Owen, leader of the Social Democratic Party, speaking at the Party's annual conference at Buxton on September 12, 1984, advocated free distribution of shares of the nationalized companies to every British citizen, and future distribution of the equity of large private companies to all citizens (*London Times*, September 13, 1984, p. 4). The SDP has several committees working on specific plans for such citizen capital ownership. Their commitment to the idea makes it probable that this will be an important issue in the next British general election.

That brings us to socialists and Marxists. Should the USOP concept appeal to them? In my opinion, they should find in USOP a fulfillment of their drive for social justice. To cure the malignancies they perceived in capitalism, Marx and Engels prescribed a simple remedy: *socialization* of MOP ownership. However, they never precisely defined what they meant by socialization. Lenin interpreted their writings as a call for government ownership and control of the means of production—nationalization. But to other influential Marxists, notably Karl Kautsky (1854-1938), who was known as "the pope of Marxism" and who actually wrote the fourth volume of *Das Kapital*, this was heresy. In his 1932 essay, "Is Soviet Russia a Socialist State?" published as part of a 1946 book entitled *Social Democracy vs. Communism*, Kautsky wrote:

> Certainly, it is the aim of Socialists to deprive the capitalists of the means of production. But that in itself is not enough. We must also determine who is to control these means of production. When another minority takes the place of the capitalists and controls the means of production, independently of the people and frequently against their will, the change in property relations thus accomplished signifies least of all Socialism....
>
> In Russia, it is the government, not the people, who controls the means of production. The government is thus the master of the people....
>
> Our duty is not merely to abolish the capitalist order but to set up a higher order in its place. But we must oppose those forces aiming to destroy capitalism only to replace it with a barbarous mode of production...What we see in Russia is, therefore, not Socialism but its antithesis. It can become Socialism only when the people expropriate the expropriators now in power, to use a Marxian expression. Thus, the socialist masses of Russia find themselves with respect to the problem of control of the means of production in the same situation which confronts the workers in capitalist countries. The fact that in Russia the expropriating expropriators call themselves Communists makes not the slightest difference. [pp. 89-90]

In this distinction between social ownership and nationalized ownership of the means of production, Kautsky was supported by leading Marxists of his time, including Rosa Luxemburg (1871-1919), who pioneered Marxism in Russia, Poland, and Germany, as well as two other pioneers, August Bebel (1840-1913), and Eduard Bernstein (1850-1932).

Socialists and Marxists should not be put off by the notion of using capitalistic devices such as credit and company shares to achieve social ownership of the means of production. Justification for their use will be found in the writings of Marx and Engels themselves. Volume Three of *Das Kapital*, completed by Engels and published in 1894, represents the last word of Marx and Engels on socialization of MOP ownership. The following excerpts from Chapter 27, "The Role of Credit in Capitalist Production," (Vintage Books edition, Random House, 1981) have a direct bearing on our search. In this excerpt, Marx and Engels perceive the great potential of the joint-stock company, England's nineteenth-century equivalent of today's publicly traded corporations:

III. Formation of joint-stock companies. This involves:

1. Tremendous expansion in the scale of production, and enterprises which would be impossible for individual capitals. At the same time, enterprises that were previously government ones became social.

2. Capital, which is inherently based on a social mode of production and presupposes a social concentration of means of production and labour-power, now receives the form of social capital (capital of directly associated individuals) in contrast to private capital, and its enterprises appear as social enterprises as opposed to private ones. This is the abolition of capital as private property within the confines of the capitalist mode of production itself.

* * *

This result of capitalist production in its highest development is a necessary point of transition towards the transformation of capital back into the property of the producers, though no longer as the private property of individual producers, but rather as their property as associated producers, as directly social property. It is furthermore a point of transition towards the transformation of all functions formerly bound up with capital ownership in the reproduction process into simple functions of the associated producers, into social functions.

* * *

This is the abolition of the capitalist mode of production within the capitalist mode of production itself, and hence a self-abolishing contradiction, which presents itself prima facie as a mere point of transition to a new form of production. [pp. 567-9]

Then Marx and Engels went on to describe how the credit system can play a role in socializing MOP ownership through joint-stock companies (corporations):

This credit system, since it forms the principal basis for the gradual transformation of capitalist private enterprises into capitalist joint-stock companies, presents in the same way the means for the gradual extension of cooperative enterprises on a more or less national scale. Capitalist joint-stock companies as much as co-operative factories should be viewed as transition forms from the capitalist mode of production to the associated one, simply that in the one case the opposition is abolished in a negative way, and in the other in a positive way.

Up till now, we have considered the development of credit—and the latent abolition of capital ownership contained within it—principally in relation to industrial capital. [pp. 571-2]

In these passages, Marx and Engels recognized that the modern corporation could be used to socialize capital ownership, because it could divide ownership (in the form of readily-transferable stock certificates) among an unlimited number of people. This was in contrast to earlier stages of capitalism, when ownership of an enterprise was solely in the hands of an individual or family. They also foresaw the role that credit could play in this transformation, by fueling the development and expansion of numerous large stock corporations, which in turn would spread capital ownership to a much broader group of people than had been owners in the more primitive stages of industrialization.

Thus, with remarkable insight, Marx and Engels perceived the potential socialization of MOP ownership through the early joint-stock company and the primitive credit system of their time. They found in these two elements, even in such crude forms, a way to overcome their basic objections to capitalism by *the latent abolition of capitalist property.*

Although Marx and Engels appreciated the potential of widespread stock ownership and broad use of credit, they could not envision any constructive or ''social'' use of these elements under capitalism. They assumed both would be used to further overconcentrate capital ownership and perpetuate class divisiveness, and thus they did not lay out any plan for use of these elements in socializing capital ownership. But what Marx and Engels failed to realize is that the credit system could be used for the benefit of noncapitalists as well as capitalists.

It seems to me that the foregoing analysis presents the Labour Party of Great Britain with an elegant solution to its long-standing ''Clause IV'' problem. Clause IV, Section IV of the Labour Party constitution commits the party to work for ''common ownership of the means of production.'' For more than half a century, this clause has caused friction and polarization within the party, especially since nationalization has been tried—without notable success—in Great Britain and other European nations. Nationalization has now gone out of style, and even the Socialist International, the descendent of Marx's First International, no longer advocates government MOP ownership. Since the framers of the Labour Party constitution did not specify government ownership, why wouldn't a democratic form of socialization, such as USOP, achieve the aim of common ownership?

USOP should appeal to the British Labour Party for another reason. They have been relatively slow to come to the support of employee ownership, largely because they perceive it as a threat to the authority and power of labor unions. The theory is that if a worker owns shares in his own company, he is less likely to need the services of labor union officials to represent him in dealing with the company, and, at least theoretically, he is less interested in pushing high pay demands which might reduce the profits and dividends he would receive as a shareholder. Supporting USOP is again an elegant way out for leaders of the Labour Party, because USOP, not being based upon the employment relationship, poses no such threat to union power.

Now that we have made USOP palatable to socialists and Marxists through use of the term "socialization," we must take care not to frighten off traditional capitalists who will have no part of socialism. Socialization is a word not much favored by Americans. It is suspect in our eyes, associated vaguely with communism and things un-American. But we must not allow such superstitions to interfere with our quest for a method of spreading the benefits of capitalism throughout our society, even though some people will see in any form of socialization evidence of a Marxist plot. This occurred when Franklin Roosevelt proposed the Social Security program, although it is now considered an integral part of welfare capitalism. Indeed, capitalism itself probably wouldn't be around any more if its harsh "survival of the fittest" philosophy had not been tempered by the adoption of Social Security and other social welfare programs.

Fortunately, major dictionaries do not limit their definitions of "socialize" to nationalization of MOP or capital ownership. *American Heritage* defines it broadly as "to convert or adapt to the needs of society." *Webster's* includes this definition: "to adapt to social needs or uses." The *Oxford Dictionary of the English Language* definition is "to make fit for living in society." Pope John Paul II, in his 1981 encyclical, *On Human Work*, defined socialization as making *each person* a part owner of the means of production (No. 14).

Please note that USOP, at least in its Kitty Hawk model, is not a scheme for redistributing the wealth of the nation. It does not redistribute present wealth, but it will distribute future wealth more equitably. It will give the disadvantaged sector of society the same access to long-term credit that has always been held exclusively by the wealthy.

Finally, you may question whether USOP is too radical a plan to be taken seriously in the political arena. USOP is radical, in that it cuts to the roots of the problems it is aimed at. If there were any easy or nonradical solutions, they would probably have been found by now. It is time for us to look beyond such palliatives and consider a solution that matches up to the staggering scope of our economic problems. Besides, after you get used to the idea that it is possible to make our capitalistic economic system consistent with our political democracy, USOP doesn't seem all that radical, does it?

Here are some political questions you may wish to consider in your essay:

Can the USOP concept be made palatable to the average American voter, as a partial substitute for wages and welfare based on democratization of credit?

Can USOP become a substitute for government intervention that satisfies the egalitarian drive of American liberals?

Can USOP help Britain's Labour Party to solve the dilemma of Clause IV, Section IV of the Labour Party constitution, which mandates "common ownership" of the means of production?

7.

AN IMPORTANT POLITICAL QUESTION: HOW CAN USOP BENEFICIARIES *EARN* THEIR SHARES?

Probably the most controversial feature of USOP is the handing out of shares in blue-chip companies to people who, unlike the present shareholders, did not earn the shares through their work (employee shares) or did not have the savings to buy the shares for cash. As one businessman friend put it to me, "How can you justify handing out stock to people who don't have to pay for it and perhaps never did a day's work in their lives; while millions of people have saved their hard-earned money to buy shares in the same companies, or have earned those shares through an employee share ownership plan? And isn't it true that people tend to put a low value on things they do not pay for? Doesn't this doom USOP to be just another government handout program that will not raise morale or have the positive effects you hope for?"

These questions are apt to be asked by politicians whose support is sought for USOP. Even liberal politicians today are wary about schemes that have the earmarks of a handout. They would support USOP much more readily if the USOP beneficiaries could *earn* their shares.

I have searched long and hard for methods by which USOP shares could be earned. My research is far from complete, and I hope that you essayists will come up with your own answers to these questions, which go to the very heart of the USOP principle. I shall set forth here my preliminary answers, as nothing more than a guideline for you to build upon.

My basic answer to the first question is that people who are able to save enough money to buy shares, and those who earn shares through their employment, would still receive those "paid" and "earned" shares, which should be worth a lot more if we have a healthy economic system that is not completely dependent upon wages and welfare. The only real change is that USOP opens long-term credit to everyone, instead of limiting it to those who need it least. This democratization of long-term credit is the operating mechanism of USOP.

This brings us to the question of what kind of capitalism we want, a question we have never faced up to, because we have never defined capitalism in any law, regulation, or constitutional provision. We have simply adopted it by osmosis as our national economic system, without setting its limits and boundaries. Indeed, we try to avoid describing the American system as capitalism, preferring buzz-words like "free enterprise."

Why can't we define American and British capitalism as a system in which everyone can participate as an owner, provided that each proposed owner does whatever is reasonably within his or her powers to earn the right to own?

Certainly each proposed owner should be required to earn the right to USOP shares by obeying the law and doing his or her best to contribute to the well-being of American society. At the time of the Homestead Act (1862), the American government decided to open capitalism to all those who wanted to earn a piece of land, which was then the principal form of capital. The objective there was not only to spread the wealth but also to get the land settled, and for that purpose the Homestead Act provided title to 160 acres to individual settlers, provided that the settler resided on the land for five years. This was in pursuit of the Jeffersonian ideal of a republic in which yeoman farmers (capital owners) own and cultivate self-sufficient, self-liquidating capital properties in the form of farmland.

Why can't we define capitalism today in the tradition of the Homestead Act, enabling all those who meet the performance requirements to become capitalists?

The first Homestead Bill was presented to Congress in 1846, but there was an endless debate about such a radical government handout. Congress finally passed a Homestead Act in 1860, but it was vetoed by President James Buchanan. Employers opposed it because they feared it would deplete the labor market and thus increase wages. But the Republican platform of 1860 promised a new Homestead Bill, and Abraham Lincoln's victory brought about its passage. He signed it into law on May 20, 1862.

It was conditioned upon behavior that was lawful and considered desirable by the U.S. Congress, because its very first sentence set up the requirement that each applicant be a citizen of the United States, at least 21 years of age or the head of a family, who has "never borne arms against the United States government or given aid and comfort to its enemies." Section 2 also made eligible those who performed service in the Army or Navy of the United States, even if they were under 21 and not the head of a family. The entry fee was $10. According to Section 2, in order to get absolute title to the land, the applicant merely had to prove by two credible witnesses that he or she resided upon or cultivated the land for five consecutive years. Since the improvement and cultivation requirements were not specific, mere squatting on the land was sufficient.

To make USOP a modern counterpart of the Homestead Act, how should we organize the activity that the USOP shareholders would be required to perform in order to earn their shares? First of all, should we require the USOP shareholders to execute promissory notes in the amount of the shares issued to them? Would such a provision really mean anything? It seems to me that the poorest and the most unscrupulous among them would readily sign the notes because they would have no property against which payment could be enforced. On the other hand, it might inhibit others who are more industrious and who feared that they might lose some of their savings or property if the USOP shares did not pay for themselves. And we would not achieve universal capitalism because there might well be millions of people who would not sign the notes.

Some would argue that since the Homestead Act distributed capital to everyone who would settle on free land, so USOP could distribute shares to all those who would participate in the economy as consumers, thereby spreading ownership and purchasing power to the area where it is most needed. But merely being a willing consumer is probably not enough to satisfy the American concept of earning your own way. In *The American Ethos: Public Attitudes Toward Capitalism and Democracy*, Herbert McClosky and John Zaller reported on extensive sampling of American public opinion on this subject:

As late as the 1970s, most Americans were still saying that the poor should "help themselves" and that the government should just let each person get ahead on his own rather than guaranteeing everyone a job and a good standard of living. Even if a person is elderly or impoverished, many Americans continue to believe that responsibility for his welfare rests principally with him and not with the government. [pp. 270-271]

* * *

Americans are, in short, willing to have society assist people who are in distress, but do not believe it has a duty to provide assistance permanently. [p. 274]

* * *

When asked whether the federal government should simply give money to needy people, Americans usually said that it should not. However, if the proposal for welfare contains a strong reference to work or its associated values, opinion reverses sharply. By margins that are sometimes very large, Americans support welfare programs that require recipients to perform useful work in order to receive aid. [p. 275]

This attitude is reflected in the strong American trend toward changing welfare into "workfare." Experimental programs in states such as California, New York, and Massachusetts, have aroused some hope that by requiring welfare recipients to seek work, they can be rerouted to the paid employment sector, through training, public service jobs, grants to employers, and other techniques. But such programs have shown little promise of creating full time employment at regular pay, simply because there is an endemic shortage of such employment in our economy. Yet, we have a vast need for *work*, as distinguished from paid employment. There is no end of useful work to be done in social services, the arts and humanities, pollution control, repair of the infrastructure—indeed, the work of humanity, as I call it. But there seems to be no feasible method of paying for this work under the present system.

During the period 1933-1941, Franklin Roosevelt's New Deal created several vehicles for performing the work of humanity: the Public Works Administration (PWA), Works Progress Administration (WPA), and the Civilian Conservation Corps (CCC). While designed primarily to provide work relief for the unemployed millions, these agencies accomplished much important work. The PWA in its time (1933-1939) built more than 70 percent of the nation's new educational buildings; 65 percent of its new courthouses, city halls, and sewage disposal plants; 35 percent of its new public health facilities; and 10 percent of its new roads, bridges and subways. During its eight-year life, the WPA put 8.5 million people to work, building more than 650,000 miles of roads, 125,000 public buildings, 75,000 bridges, 8,000 parks, and 800 airports. Projects in the arts employed thousands of writers, actors, and artists. The CCC employed young men from families on relief in reforestation and other environmental projects, helping to stem the soil erosion that created the dust bowl.

All of these agencies disappeared when America entered World War II, and were never reactivated. Why not? Because we had faith in the ability of the private sector economy to reach full employment; because there is a liberal bias against forced work; and because the conservatives among us believe that it is cheaper simply to give the poor a welfare check than for the taxpayers to maintain workfare bureaucracies and to shoulder the nonlabor costs (materials, design, supervision, etc.) of the work they do.

The addition of USOP to this equation opens exciting vistas. Granted that public service work is more expensive than welfare handouts if wages must be paid. But suppose that instead of wages for public service work, the recipients were made eligible for the wages of capital, in the form of dividends from USOP shares—would this change in the source of payment enable us to recreate the achievements of the WPA and the CCC in a way that is economically and politically feasible?

Such jobs would still carry some of the makework stigma of the WPA, but working as an owner of corporate shares rather than as a recipient of public handouts should make a big difference, in my opinion. Wealthy men and women do lots of dirty chores in their own gardens and stables. And there are many stories about the CCC boys of the depression days who felt they owned the trees they had planted, and went back years later to see them grown tall.

Here, then, is the embryo of a monumental idea. We could give welfare recipients two choices: they could remain on welfare, with payments cut to the lowest level consistent with responsible government; or, they could work their way out of welfare by moving into the USOP program, earning their shares by avoiding criminal activity and doing assigned tasks in the work of humanity. And we could accomplish the work of humanity economically because we would not have to pay the wages of welfare to the USOP shareholders.

An experimental program now under way in Florida and Missouri may furnish a precedent for this new approach to public service work. Edgar Cahn, a law professor at the University of Miami, devised a plan whereby senior citizens in good health are able to earn "service credits" by doing volunteer work to help other seniors. Cahn describes his plan as "a mix between the blood bank concept and a state-operated barter system. Like a blood bank, participants can build up credits against future need; like a barter system, it allows participants to purchase services without cash.'' As enacted in Florida, the plan allows people 60 years or over to perform homemaker care for the elderly, which earns them service credits that will be accepted as payment for like services when their own time of need arrives. This is a break with the past method of paying for such services from savings, insurance, or public funds. It can harness some of the enormous energy of our ''surplus'' people and greatly facilitate the work of humanity, with negligible cost to the state.

For an illuminating discussion of the work of humanity and maintenance of work incentive, see the remarks of Professor Ronald Dore, quoted in Section 10 below.

Please consider these ideas as you plan your essay. We need a great deal of research and creative thinking on how the USOP shareholders can earn their shares, and how such a program can improve American and British society by accomplishing the work of humanity.

8.

BUILDING ON EMPLOYEE OWNERSHIP

As we saw in Section 2, expansion of employee share ownership cannot produce universal capitalism, and therefore it does not furnish the answer to the essay problem. However, it is a highly developed and rapidly growing force in the economy which provides an ideal cornerstone for universal share ownership. Therefore, let us consider the present state of employee share ownership, starting with the United States.

The idea of workers owning shares in the enterprise that employs them is even older than Marxism. In 1826, German economist Johann Heinrich von Thunen wrote a book on this subject called *The Isolated State*. Von Thunen, however, did not confine himself to theoretical speculation. He owned large agricultural estates, and he applied his theories to his own farm workers, paying them the prevailing wages, and in addition, agreeing to share his profits with them. But instead of paying these profit-sharing bonuses in cash, he reinvested this money in equipment that would improve his farms' productivity. Each employee had an individual account to which his share of the profit was credited each year. The interest on this share was paid out annually in cash to the worker, and when the worker retired or left von Thunen's employment, he received his share of ownership in cash.

During the nineteenth and twentieth centuries, von Thunen's idea was carried on through many types of profit-sharing and ownership-sharing schemes within individual companies throughout Europe and the United States. There are many individual success stories, notably the Sears Roebuck and Eastman Kodak profit-sharing plans, which invested their funds mainly in stock of the employer company; this made the employees, at least indirectly, owners of substantial shares in the company for which they worked.

Worker ownership is an attractive idea: it seems to provide a logical incentive for increasing productivity, and it dampens the fires of class struggle by giving workers a stake in maximizing company profits. The concept of broadening worker ownership of the employer company is something like motherhood and apple pie, and therefore regularly finds its way into the platform statements of both the Democratic and Republican parties. But these boilerplate political endorsements don't say much about how worker ownership is to be created. Therefore, let's look at the specific plans that have been used for this purpose.

ESOP and Other Worker Ownership Plans

Government-subsidized worker ownership in the United States began in 1928, when Congress enacted special tax benefits designed to encourage the use of profit-sharing and stock bonus plans to provide workers with retirement income. (Note that the American employee share ownership plans, unlike some of the British and European models, are strictly retirement plans, with no benefits payable until employment has been terminated.) These tax laws allowed companies a business tax deduction for their contributions to such a plan; at the same time, the plan's income was sheltered from federal taxes until workers received the cash value of their vested benefits upon retiring or otherwise leaving the company's employ. With a few notable exceptions, such as Sears and Eastman Kodak, these profit-sharing plans diversified their portfolios, rather than investing solely in shares of the employer company. And while diversified profit-sharing plans were adopted by numerous companies, the stock bonus plan, which was enacted as a means of issuing employer stock to employees, was rarely used until 1973. Since then it has provided the foundation for Senator Russell B. Long's crusade for stock ownership plans (SOPs). He was aided by the pioneering work of Louis O. Kelso, a San Francisco lawyer who managed to install successful working models of employee share ownership even before the tax laws were amended to accomodate them.

Convinced that broadening stock ownership was the best way to ward off the threat of socialism, Senator Long, then chairman of the Senate Finance Committee, used his great influence to enact legislation authorizing a series of stock ownership plans. According to the cover story in *Business Week* of April 15, 1985, some 7,000 American companies have installed SOPs, covering nearly 10 million employees. The most important SOPs are the ESOP (Employee Stock Ownership Plan), the TRASOP (Tax Reduction Act Stock Ownership Plan), and the PAYSOP (Payroll-Based Stock Ownership Plan).

ESOP is the most widely used of these plans, and is financed by employer contributions, which are used to buy stock of the employer company. The stock is then held in trust for employees. Generally, shares are allocated on the basis of each employee's relative wage, but some companies do make equal contributions for all employees, regardless of their compensation. Employees receive this stock only after their employment has been terminated. As with other employee benefit plans that qualify for tax benefits under the Internal Revenue Code, ESOPs must be established and operated for the benefit of the employee participants.

Lawyers and corporate financiers have developed some sophisticated uses of ESOPs, the most prominent of which is the "leveraged" ESOP, so called because it involves use of bank loans to buy employer stock. This enables ESOPs to buy large blocks of shares on the installment plan—something that trustees of other employee benefit plans cannot do. Also, it provides the biggest advantage of ESOPs from the corporate standpoint: It enables the employer to take a tax deduction for payment of both the principal and the interest on the money borrowed by the ESOP to buy the corporation's shares. Interest is always a tax-deductible expense for corporations, just as it is on your personal income tax return. But repayment of the loan *principal* is never a tax-deductible expense, for individuals or corporations, unless a corporation has a leveraged ESOP.

The ESOP doesn't actually give the company a tax deduction for principal payments, but it has the same effect. The company makes tax-deductible contributions to the ESOP, and the ESOP uses these contributions to pay off the loan principal and interest. Therefore, the expenditure that is usually called "nondeductible repayment of loan principal" is changed to "deductible contribution to ESOP."

To illustrate the leveraged ESOP, let's assume Peerless Pizza wishes to raise $1 million through that device. First, Peerless would adopt an ESOP, get it approved by the Internal Revenue Service as a qualified employee benefit plan, and then set up a trust as part of the plan. Then Peerless would arrange a loan of $1 million from its bank. The loan is actually made to the ESOP trust rather than to Peerless, but Peerless guarantees that the loan will be repaid. Peerless's employees are not responsible for repaying the loan; only the ESOP trust and Peerless sign the note. Now the Peerless ESOP trust is holding $1 million lent by the bank, which it has to repay, let's say, in five annual installments of $200,000 each, with interest. The ESOP trust then uses the $1 million bank loan to buy $1 million worth of newly issued stock from Peerless at market value. The ESOP holds this stock in trust for the employees of Peerless, who will receive shares in proportion to their salaries when they retire or leave the company. Peerless makes an annual contribution to the ESOP to cover the principal and interest payments on the bank loan. Its maximum tax-deductible contribution to the ESOP would be 25 percent of its payroll. Since Peerless's payroll is over $100 million, it can contribute as much as $25 million per year and get a tax deduction. To repay the bank loan (including interest) for its ESOP, Peerless would have to make contributions of about $300,000 per year for five years, well within the 25 percent of payroll allowed by tax law.

This plan would enable Peerless to repay the entire principal and interest of the $1 million loan with tax-deductible contributions to the ESOP. If Peerless had received a simple $1 million bank loan without using an ESOP, it would have had to repay the principal with after-tax funds, and so would have had to earn a lot more than $1 million in profits to repay $1 million.

However, leveraged ESOPs are not considered advantageous for large, profitable companies since the company must repay a bank loan in addition to diluting its stock by issuing shares to the ESOP, thereby in effect paying twice for the same $1 million financing. Leveraged ESOPs are used mostly by smaller companies or those having a special reason for issuing a large block of new shares, such as warding off an unfriendly takeover attempt or getting rid of an unprofitable division by selling it outright to employees.

ESOPs are sometimes used when the federal government steps in to bail out a troubled corporation. For example, under the Chrylser Corporation Loan Guarantee Act of 1979, Chrysler was required to set up an ESOP and contribute approximately $40 million a year until the trust's assets totaled $162.5 million of Chrysler stock, to be divided among the company's 94,000 American and Canadian employees. This stipulation was the work of Senator Long, who believes that whenever the government is called upon to bail out a corporation, the benefit should not all go to its creditors and stockholders but should also make the workers part owners, even though their ownership does not take effect until they retire or otherwise leave the company.

One of the offshoots of ESOP was the TRASOP program, which Senator Long pushed through in the Tax Reduction Act (TRA) of 1975. In effect, TRASOP enables a company to take an additional 1 percent investment tax credit, over and above the 10 percent credit allowed for the purchase of new capital items, *provided* that an amount equivalent to this 1 percent tax credit is contributed to a Tax Reduction Act Stock Ownership Plan (TRASOP) and used to buy employer stock.

To illustrate the TRASOP, let's go back to the new factory that Peerless Pizza built at a cost of $10 million. The tax laws allow Peerless an investment tax credit of 10 percent, or $1 million, for building the plant. In addition, if Peerless elected to establish a TRASOP, it could take an additional tax credit of 1 percent of the value of the new plant—$100,000—if the money was contributed to a TRASOP and used to buy Peerless stock. The $100,000 contribution would be made to a trust established under the TRASOP, which would buy $100,000 worth of Peerless stock for its employees. And like an ESOP, that stock would be distributed to employees in proportion to their salaries when they retired or left the company.

From a corporate perspective, TRASOP is more attractive than ESOP because the 1 percent tax *credit* is more valuable than the tax *deduction* permitted under ESOP. A tax deduction is merely subtracted from gross income, but a tax credit is subtracted directly from the taxes payable by Peerless, and thus amounts to a gift from the Treasury to Peerless. In effect, the tax credit means the U.S. Treasury foots the bill for stock presented to employees. And because TRASOPs cost the employer nothing, large successful companies have used TRASOPs to a much greater extent than ESOPs.

Capital-intensive industries such as oil and timber were among the first to take advantage of TRASOP. In fact, the plan's chief weakness is that it favors employees of capital-intensive companies because the tax credits and the amount of stock the employees receive are based on the size of capital outlays. To remove this bias, Senator Long engineered an amendment to the 1981 tax laws, which linked tax credits and employer contributions to a percentage of a company's payroll rather than a percentage of its capital outlays. The amended tax credit plan, known as PAYSOP, went into effect in January of 1983. It allows a credit equivalent to one-half of 1 percent of the payroll. So, right now, Peerless Pizza, with its annual payroll of $100 million, could contribute $500,000 a year to a PAYSOP trust (one-half of 1 percent) and receive a tax credit for the entire amount.

TRASOP was phased out on December 31, 1982, in favor of PAYSOP, which will remain in effect until December 31, 1987. TRA-SOP and PAYSOP are now known as "tax credit ESOPs."

Please note that the foregoing discussion relates to tax-advantaged share ownership plans. There is nothing to prevent an employer from paying bonuses or sharing profits with any of its employees, either in cash payments or in stock. In either case, the employer will receive a tax deduction for paying that extra compensation, just as the employer receives a tax deduction for the regular payroll. But the employees would have to pay income tax immediately on cash or shares received in that way, unless the payment was made under a "qualified" tax-deductible plan. In order to qualify, such plans (whether pension, profit-sharing, stock bonus, or ESOP) must include all employees, and the benefits cannot be received by the employees until they retire or terminate the employment. As a practical matter, ESOPs have emerged as the dominant method of making employees owners, because of the tax advantages to both employers and employees which Senator Long and his colleagues engineered.

Employee Ownership in Great Britain

Serious development of employee ownership in Britain dates from 1958, when the pioneering work, *The Challenge of Employee Shareholding*, was published by Dr. George Copeman. In contrast to the American ESOPs, the British schemes do not universally require that all employees be included, and they are not necessarily retirement plans. The retirement function in Great Britain is left largely to pension schemes and Social Security, with employee share ownership occupying a middle ground between current compensation and pension benefits.

The broadest British plan is called the Profit-Sharing Scheme, as approved under the Finance Act of 1978, amended by the Finance Acts of 1980, 1982, and 1983. It is the only British plan that requires inclusion of substantially all employees, as does the American ESOP. A share of company profits (not to exceed 5 percent of total profits as mandated by the Investment Protection Committees of the British Insurance Association and the National Association of Pension Funds) is paid over to trustees who purchase shares of the company on behalf of the participating employees. All full-time employees with five or more years of service must be eligible to participate. Distribution must be "on similar terms," which means that the shares allocated to each employee must be related to pay and/or length of service, or equal shares for every employee. Each participating employee is bound in contract not to sell, assign, or otherwise dispose of shares for at least two years from the date of their issuance.

As to the tax position, the employing company of course receives corporation tax relief for the money appropriated to buy these shares. Participating employees are not subject to income tax when the shares are issued. If the employee sells shares within two to seven years of the date of receipt, the employee will be subject to income tax on a descending percentage of the value of the shares, starting at 100 percent after two years, and going down to zero after seven years. In other words, employees pay no income tax whatsoever on the sale of their shares provided that they are held for seven years. If sold between two and seven years, some tax will be paid.

This scheme was originally enacted by a Labour Government in 1978, with considerable prodding from the Liberal Party, which was then in coalition with the Labour Party. It was made more attractive by legislative amendments under the Conservatives in 1980, 1982, and 1983. As of June 1985, Chancellor of the Exchequer Nigel Lawson reported that the number of these plans had risen from 30 in 1979 to around 900 presently, with some 750,000 employees participating.

The Finance Act of 1980 established a Savings Related Share Option Scheme. As in the profit-sharing scheme, virtually all employees must be eligible to participate. But participation in this plan requires the employee to enter into a SAYE (Save As You Earn) contract with either a building society or the Department for National Savings. This binds the participant for a period of five years to save a fixed sum of between £10 and £100 each month. At the end of five years, a bonus equal to 14 of the savings installments (23.3 percent) is added to the total sum saved. If the participant chooses to leave the funds in the SAYE account for a further two years, a further 14-installment bonus is added. Upon entering into the SAYE contract, the participant receives an option to subscribe for shares to the value of the sum saved, at a price equal to the market value of the shares at the date the option is granted, or a lesser figure but not less than 90 percent of that market price. The option may be exercised either when the SAYE contract matures after five years, or after seven years, if the second bonus is chosen. Thus, if the value of the shares increases over the five- or seven-year period, the participant can buy these shares very favorably through the SAYE plan at a price below the market price at the time the option is exercised. The employee is subject to capital gains tax when the shares are sold, but there is an exclusion of up to £5,600 of annual gain which is not taxable. While all employees must be eligible to participate, obviously this is a voluntary plan that depends upon the ability of individual employees to use their own savings, albeit on an advantageous basis, to buy shares in the employer company.

The third basic type of tax-relieved British plan is the Discretionary Share Option Scheme as approved under the Finance Act of 1984. Unlike the previously described option scheme, this one may include only selected individual employees whom the company management wishes to favor with options to purchase shares at advantageous prices. Thus, in practice it is a tool for encouraging and rewarding management rather than large groups of employees. The option price must not be manifestly less than the market value of the shares at the date that the option is granted. To be eligible for tax relief, the options must not be exercisable earlier than three years nor later than ten years after the date of grant. The employee pays no tax when the option is received or exercised. Tax is payable when and if the employee sells shares which he or she has acquired by the exercise of an option, but the taxes are payable at favorable capital gains rates and then only if they exceed the annual exemption of £5,600.

Under the Finance Acts of 1983 and 1984, there is also tax relief for the interest on loans used by employees to acquire shares in a company which is or will become majority-owned by employees. The movement toward majority and total employee ownership has been stronger in Great Britain than in the United States, inspired to some degree by the success of the Mondragon model. The group of Mondragon worker-owned producer cooperatives in the Basque section of Spain has chalked up an impressive record of successful operations during the past 25 years, both in the growth and recession phases of the Spanish economy. In Britain, this cooperative movement has taken several forms: the John Lewis partnership, which operated a chain of successful department stores from 1929 to 1970 as a copartnership, and since 1970 under common ownership by all employees, who share the profits through an annual cash bonus on wages; the National Freight Consortium, a collection of over 50 transport and warehousing operations, operated by the government as a nationalized company until 1982, at which time employees and pensioners bought more than 80 percent of the shares and turned the company into a very successful private business; and the "copartnership" variation illustrated by the gas companies.

In the nineteenth century, before they were nationalized, several British gas companies introduced copartnership as a method of securing employee loyalty and increasing productivity. Each employee was known as a copartner, sharing in the company's success according to a formula which allocated three-quarters of certain profits to reducing the price of gas, one-eighth to shareholder dividends, and one-eighth to employee bonuses. In some of the companies, the employee bonus was used to buy shares, which could not be sold until the employee left the company. In some instances, the worker copartners had the right to elect some directors, and also had considerable say in management decisions affecting the workplace. Harry Ball-Wilson, one of the British pioneers of wider share ownership, believes strongly in the copartnership model. Active in the field since 1950 when he first became Parliamentary Liberal Candidate for Bermondsey, Mr. Ball-Wilson commends reference to a 1913 book, *Copartnership in Industry* by C.R. Fay. Mr. Ball-Wilson plans to organize a 1989 international conference in Paris to commemorate the one-hundredth anniversary of the meeting there that inspired the copartnership movement in the British gas industry. More information on cooperative and copartnership arrangements in Great Britain will be found in *Employee Ownership—Why, How?* by Job Ownership Ltd.; *Shares for Employees* by Robert Heller; and *The Crisis for Western Political Economy* by Peter Jay.

The three basic British tax-advantaged share schemes are discussed in illuminating detail in *Shared Ownership*, by George Copeman, Peter Moore, and Carol Arrowsmith, which also describes employee share schemes in France, Germany, and other European nations. Two of the authors, George Copeman and Carol Arrowsmith, were kind enough to write a special section for this handbook, "How and Why People Build Capital," which you will find at Appendix C.

Building on This Foundation Toward Universal Share Ownership

750,000 Britons and 10 million Americans are already owners of employee shares, and employee share ownership receives across-the-board political support in both nations. How, then, can we build on this foundation to achieve our goal of universal share ownership?

One way suggests itself immediately, growing out of the principal shortcoming of employee ownership. ESOPs and similar plans have been criticized because they tend to put all the workers' eggs in one basket. This is especially true in the United States, where it is not uncommon for an ESOP to be substituted for a pension plan, thus making the retirement nest egg of the employees, as well as their living standard during their working lives, dependent on the financial performace of the employing company. Commentators from the political left, right, and center have pointed out this shortcoming. But USOP could overcome this problem by providing that, under certain conditions, ESOP shares and the like could be converted to USOP shares. This would give employees the lifetime security that is missing in the ESOP-type scheme. It would also make employee ownership much more saleable to employees, for then employers could bargain for the substitution of ESOPs for pension plans without endangering the future security of the employees.

Such a convertibility feature would give a tremendous boost to employee ownership. One question to be addressed in the essay competition is how the convertibility feature should be designed. Naturally, we would want to encourage the most beneficial type of ESOP, the kind that truly benefits the employees at least as much as it benefits the insiders who control the business. What conditions should be put on convertibility? At what times and in what ratios could ESOP shares be converted to USOP shares? And how could we guard against dilution of the USOP fund by conversion of worthless or near-worthless ESOP shares into USOP shares?

The convertibility feature actually has two important facets. Number one, it serves as a safety net for those employees who are depending upon ESOP shares in their retirement years; and number two, it is a potential means of getting the best out of ESOPs by limiting convertibility to those plans that contain the features we desire to encourage in the future development of employee ownership.

Beyond convertibility, is there any other way that we can hook up employee ownership with the USOP concept, so as to benefit both groups? Obviously, ESOP is a stepping-stone to USOP. Philosophically, ideologically, and politically, it has laid the foundation for universal share ownership. How else can we build on that foundation?

9.

SYNTHESIS WITH SOCIAL SECURITY AND PENSION PLANS

I hope that an ideal plan of universal capital ownership will emerge from these essay contests. The ideal plan should probably include a synthesis of several forms of ownership, income, and security. The whole area of pensions, for example, is related to capital ownership, even though the rights held by workers in pension plans do not actually make them owners of corporate stock. Then there are the existing capital ownership schemes based on employment, such as profit-sharing plans, ESOPs, TRASOPs, and PAYSOPs. In addition, Social Security and government transfer payments should be synthesized with USOP so that benefits do not overlap and recipients are given an incentive to progress from the welfare system to participation in capitalism. And the insurance industry should be encouraged to synthesize present and future forms of life insurance with USOP.

The precarious future financial position of Social Security systems, both in the United States and Great Britain, is well known. An effective USOP program that provided every household with substantial income from capital ownership would, of course, ease the strain on Social Security and eventually make it possible for government to phase it out. There are immediate opportunities to synthesize the strengths of Social Security with the new stream of income that would become available from USOP, to the benefit of both.

In this connection, Stuart M. Butler in his 1985 book, *Privatizing Federal Spending: A Strategy to Eliminate the Deficit*, suggests that the Social Security system could be, at least partially, privatized. He believes that Social Security should be split into two distinct parts: a welfare element and a social insurance element. The welfare element would be financed from general taxation, as in the case of other welfare programs. The social insurance element would be financed according to normal actuarial principles, with payroll-related contributions and benefits strictly related to those contributions. This latter portion—the social insurance element—need not be operated by the federal government; it is a pure insurance system that could be transferred to the private sector. A detailed plan for such a privatized Social Security system was prepared by Peter Ferrara as detailed in his 1982 book, *Social Security Reform*. Ferrara likens the pure insurance function of Social Security to an expanded version of the Individual Retirement Account (IRA). To the privatizing concepts of Butler and Ferrara should be added the possible systhesis of the Social Security system with USOP, thus making it easier to privatize portions of Social Security.

Great Britain is ahead of the United States in this respect in that it has partly privatized Social Security. In 1978, Britain embarked on a comprehensive opting-out plan with the support of both major parties, and now has a two-tiered Social Security system. The first tier is mandatory and provides a basic minimum pension. The second tier provides a pension based on earnings and is voluntary. Private companies, not individuals, can opt out of this tier if they establish a plan for their workers at least as good as the state system. Since 1978, more than 45 percent of all workers have contracted out of the second tier. The opting-out program has strong union support, and has substantially reduced the British government's Social Security expense. (See John C. Goodman, *Social Security in the United Kingdom: Contracting Out of the System*; John C. Goodman, ''Private Alternatives to Social Security: The Experience of Other Countries.'')

Pensions are an even more promising area of synthesis since they are already privatized and voluntary on the part of non-governmental employers. Pension funds in the United States today absorb one hundred billion dollars in new contributions each year, and the estimated total of fund dollars is one-and-a-quarter trillion dollars. This is just slightly less than the national debt, and by the year 2000, the total will increase to more than four trillion dollars in pension funds. By that time, the total pension funds will represent majority ownership of all the common stock in America. But, as we have seen, this does not expand capital ownership, since pensions are strictly a retirement benefit and they do not confer ownership status on the beneficiaries.

They represent funds that workers have earned and in some cases have actually contributed to.

Along with Social Security and pensions, essayists should consider how life insurance could be synthesized with USOP.

10.

OTHER PLANS TO CONSIDER

In addition to the Kitty Hawk model and others previously mentioned, there are several specific plans that you may want to consider in connection with your essay.

The National Dividend Plan was proposed by Florida industrialist John H. Perry, Jr. in his 1964 book, *The National Dividend*. Perry has refined the plan during the last twenty years and has spent over $7 million promoting it. The thrust of the plan is to take the collections from the corporate income tax and place them in a National Dividend Trust Fund. From this fund, a yearly check would be issued to every registered voter, once the federal budget is balanced. These dividends would be tax-free. Every year that the budget fell out of balance and into deficit, the money in the National Dividend Trust Fund would be used to reduce the deficit instead of being distributed to the registered voters. This would give every voter a vested interest in resisting federal deficits—no balanced budget, no national dividend check. After many years of effort by a qualified professional staff, finally Perry was able to get his National Dividend Plan into proposed legislation, in the form of H.R. 56, "a bipartisan proposal for national profit-sharing." As of this writing, the bill has not come out of committee nor been put to a vote.

For our purposes, the plan need not be tied to the separate issue of the balanced budget. We could consider the possibility of collecting the corporate income tax and paying it out to the registered voters in equal shares. This would give each voter approximately $400 to $500 per year, since there are about 110,000,000 registered American voters, and the corporate income tax raises about $50 billion per year. In my opinion, this would not accomplish any of the major purposes of USOP, other than a token step toward allowing the little people to share in the profits earned by corporate giants. But it has the advantage of simplicity, and it might be a way of opening the door to USOP. Certainly, Mr. Perry is to be commended for his dedication to the difficult task of promoting economic change. If you want further information, write to: John H. Perry, Jr., Americans for the National Dividend Act, Inc., 1901 N. Ft. Myer Drive, 12th Floor, Rosslyn, VA 22209.

A more sweeping concept is the National Mutual Fund, as proposed by Dr. James S. Albus in *People's Capitalism: The Economics of the Robot Revolution.* Dr. Albus, an internationally recognized authority on industrial robotics with the National Bureau of Standards, proposes creation of a semiprivate investment corporation called the National Mutual Fund. NMF would use money borrowed from the Federal Reserve to make stock purchases from private industry. This increased availability of investment funds would stimulate the economy and increase productivity. Profits from these investments would be paid to the general public in the form of dividends, making every adult citizen a capitalist to that extent. Dr. Albus estimates that per capita income from the NMF would reach $6,000 a year within 25 years, assuming successful investment of the money available.

Since Dr. Albus visualizes the NMF as a source of additional investment funds for industry, he is concerned about its possible inflationary impact. To counteract this, he has designed a "demand regulation policy," through which savings from consumers would be temporarily withheld so as to prevent disposable income from rising before productivity gains from NMF investments were actually realized. This withholding scheme would be designed so that low-income people would be less affected and they would earn interest in excess of current inflation.

Dr. Albus's concept has been supported by the Social Credit movement in Great Britain and in New Zealand. His book, *People's Capitalism*, is well worth reading and his National Mutual Fund idea deserves careful consideration. In my opinion, it would not conflict with USOP and it might be developed as an adjunct to the USOP concept, particularly to overcome the criticism of the Kitty Hawk model that it favors the large established companies over promising companies with new ideas and new products.

Another scheme is the Capital Formation Plan developed by the

Sabre Foundation and described in its 1972 publication, *Expanded Ownership*, which was edited by John McClaughry. The Capital Formation Plan aims to stimulate greater use of equity financing and to encourage low and middle-income individuals, not just employees, to purchase shares through tax incentives. Specifically, all people with annual incomes below $20,000 could take a tax deduction for the amount they invest in corporate stock up to $3,000. To encourage firms to engage in greater equity financing, a split rate corporate income tax schedule would be adopted, through which retained earnings would be taxed much more heavily than those that are distributed. To encourage companies to sell their new equity issues to the capital formation funds (CFF) from which the individuals would buy their diversified stock portfolio, dividends paid on shares sold to a CFF would be tax-deductible. The revenue loss to the Treasury, though substantial in the early years, would be gradually offset by the increased income taxes on dividends received and also by the reduction in the amount of interest deductions taken by companies.

In some respects, the Capital Formation Plan resembles the French Loi Monory, or Monory Laws, named after the scheme established by M. Rene Monory in France in 1978. Basically, the Loi Monory is a form of tax incentive to encourage individuals to invest in equities either directly or through specifically designed funds. The objectives were to improve the equity base of the corporate sector, especially in the face of rising interest rates that inhibited capital expenditures; to strengthen the role of the stock market; to lure the private investor away from traditional investments such as savings banks and building society accounts—which are basically short-term investments—toward a long-term commitment to trade and industry; and to reverse the ever-increasing percentage of share ownership gobbled up by institutions as opposed to individuals.

Under the original 1978 scheme, each French household was allowed to deduct from taxable income up to 5,000 francs per year of new net investment in shares of French companies. Individuals could buy shares directly through the Bourse (the French stock exchange), or units in specially designated funds called Monory Sicavs, provided the funds maintained at least 60 percent of their portfolio in French equities. In 1983, this scheme was succeeded by one known as the Loi Delors, under which the tax credit was reduced to 25 percent of purchase price, but its limits were increased from 5,000 French francs to 10,000 francs, with an allowance of 14,000 francs for a married couple. In order to qualify, the investment must be a fresh one rather than based on proceeds of sale of shares in an existing portfolio. The investment must be held for at least four years and it must be in the shares of French companies or in the special Monory Sicavs with 60 percent French equity.

The Loi Monory and similar plans in Belgium, Sweden, and Norway have been fairly successful in adding new shareholders, increasing equity investment in business, and causing share prices to rise. However, the plan as proposed in Great Britain was opposed by the Thatcher government for the reasons given in the following statement of Lord Brabazon of Tara in a House of Lords debate on February 20, 1985:

> Many noble Lords have mentioned the Loi Monory and its successor and have called upon the Government to introduce measures akin to those operating in France. The Government have considered this possibility seriously and there are some attractions. But I am afraid that there are also a number of disadvantages and these outweigh the advantages. First, creating a new category of priviliged savings would carry with it the same difficulties that would be involved in extending the Business Expansion Scheme qualification to quoted companies. There would be a blunting of the incentives currently available for investment in small, unquoted companies—which have the greatest need for risk capital and the greatest problems in getting it.
>
> Secondly, if the take-up was worthwhile, it would cost a lot of money. If the limit was, say £1,000 per year, the cost would be between £300 million and £400 million per year for every million taxpayers who invested. It would also add substantially to Inland Revenue staff numbers. Thirdly, and most important, introducing such a general relief would create a new class of privileged savings and be quite contrary to the Government's policy of reducing distortions in the tax system. Last year, the Investment Income Surcharge and Life Assurance Premium Relief were withdrawn to remove biases which discriminated against direct investment in shares. It would be rather perverse and against the general grain of policy to introduce a new fiscal distortion a year later.

The Capital Formation Plan was the basis for legislation proposed by President Gerald Ford in 1976, known as BSOP (Broadened Stock Ownership Plan). The general idea of BSOP was to allow every person a tax deduction of up to 15 percent of earned income with a maximum deduction of $1,500, for buying shares that would be held for a minimum of seven years. The maximum deduction of $1,500 would be available only to those with earned income below $20,000. For those with income from $20,000 to $40,000, the benefits would gradually reduce, reaching zero at $40,000. If the shares were held for seven years and then sold, the proceeds would be taxed as capital gains; but if any were sold before seven years, gains would be taxed as ordinary income.

Some critics dubbed BSOP "the Stockbrokers' Relief Act of 1976," since it would increase sales of shares and probably drive up the market price because more people would bid against each other for the existing public supply of shares, and then they would be holding on to these shares for seven years to get the tax advantages of BSOP. Other critics of BSOP said that it probably would not result in new savings but would merely shift savings from bank accounts into the stock market. BSOP, in any event, did not capture the imagination of Congress. It was voted down in the Senate Finance Committee and was killed on the floor of the Senate in 1976.

The Individual Retirement Account (IRA), enacted by Congress in 1982, has some of the attributes of the Capital Formation Plan. An IRA may be established by an individual who is not covered by any other qualified plan established by an employer. Tax-deductible contributions are limited to the lesser of 15 percent of earnings or $2,000 per year. However, unlike the Capital Formation Plan, no distribution can be made from an IRA until the person establishing the account dies, is disabled, or reaches age 59 1/2. There is also the Keogh Plan, a form of qualified retirement plan covering self-employed individuals, who may contribute up to 15 percent of net earnings to a maximum of $7,500 per year on a tax-deductible basis.

Plans to stimulate the purchase of shares through tax relief have some merit, but it is clear that since they benefit only those who have savings, they would not bring the structural changes that we are searching for, nor would they make every Briton or every American an owner as required by the essay topic. Nevertheless, they deserve your attention because they may contain elements which could be worked into the ideal plan for universal capital ownership.

Professor James E. Meade of Cambridge University, the 1977 Nobel Laureate in Economics, has been shaping his plans for "labour-capital partnerships" and a "social dividend" in recent years. The latest statement of these ideas is in his 1985 paper, "Wage-Fixing Revisited." All British essayists should consult that paper and the other Meade references in the bibliography section of this handbook. Professor Meade is also completing a new book on this subject which may be in print before the essay competition deadline of December 31, 1986.

In his T.H. Marshall Memorial Lecture at the University of Southampton on March 14, 1985, Professor Ronald P. Dore of the Technical Change Centre in London, put forward a plan for a social dividend of the type originally suggested by Professor James Meade. The specifics of his plan are as follows:

> The scheme I am about to outline takes off from the Meade ideas just noted. It tries to deal with the transition problem and in a way that takes account of the concentration of unemployment among the younger age groups. First of all, to begin with the least important part, why not build up the State Patrimony, the capital fund from which the social dividend is to be paid, gradually and in kind—by the process of capital dilution. Companies dilute their equity by giving the Fund a free rights issue equal to x per cent of their existing equity every year. The Fund could likewise acquire an x divided by 100 + x share in the ownership title to real estate and art objects valued over a certain sum, that share to be realized whenever the item changes hands. In this way, the fund could slowly build up. If the dilution were two percent, the funds would acquire half the national wealth in 36 years, three-quarters in 72 years.
>
> The more important part of the idea is the counterpart of the slow buildup; the slow addition to the number of beneficiaries, age group by age group. Let all those who reach the age of 16 next year receive a social dividend, a variable sum depending on the profitability of the fund's equity holdings, but also age related, perhaps by some compulsory savings device, so that it builds up over three, or if possible, five years from a teenager dividend to a full adult dividend at, say, something like 40 percent of the average wage—a good deal more for a couple with two children than the 62 percent of average wage provided by supplementary benefit now. The following year, the 17 year olds and the 16 year olds would be covered, and so on until, in about 80 years time, we have special telly programmes to mark the death of the last unendowed man, or more likely woman, with pictures of her drawing the last old-regime pension. With the endowment the teenager receives the right to study, the right to work, but also duties of unpaid community service, duties which are compulsory and universal, though widely flexible in form. Only in this way can one achieve, what all the schemes for voluntary youth community service cannot achieve—namely a genuine sharing in community work, on equal terms both of motivation and performance, between the bright ones for whom community work is an interruption in preparation for a rewarding work career, and those for whom the alternative would be unemployment.

Some implications

The variability of the dividend depending on national profitability would provide everyone with an additional incentive to take part in the producing economy, over and above the wages they might receive. An enormous free-rider problem, you will say. No-one will be able to believe that his own contribution makes a measurable impact on his own dividend. True indeed, and that means that everyone *does* have a strong interest in stopping everybody else from being a free-rider. Hence we shall see the schools suddenly revitalizing the ethic of duty and responsibility, which will not be at all a bad thing.

The overall reduction of wages which increases work opportunities would take place gradually as new age groups come on to the market. What the Young Workers' Scheme tries to do, selectively to bring down youth wages, would happen as a result of the manner of the Scheme's introduction, and within a few years, the concentration of unemployment among the young would end. The low wage cure for youth unemployment would inevitably lead to displacement of some older workers at first, but safeguards and compensating devices could be devised. What would have to go would be trade union insistence on the market principle of equal pay for equal work, which in any case is exclusively applied to manual workers in our society. The magnitude of the changeover to the endowment scheme should help us through the revolutionary change which Japan went through many decades ago, of putting everybody, not just middle class workers, on incremental scales. Can we afford, yet, to have an economy in which choosing to do one's own thing in modest poverty is wholly compatible with citizen dignity, a society in which the material incentive to work is much reduced? That was Tom Marshall's major concern in 1949. At a time when full employment had been established, by means which we thought would work forever, he did not foresee our minimum dignity problem. He wondered, though, whether people would put their backs into their jobs if income guarantees became too strong—whether, in Mandeville's terms, there was anything but their wants which could stir workers up to be serviceable. He sought hope in the thought that increasingly the search for status and for the intrinsic satisfactions of work replace Mandeville's wants as means of stirring us up. A far higher proportion of the jobs that remain today permits the mobilization of those motives than ever before. At the same time the vast array of fascinating gadgetry and travel and holiday possibilities which our new technologies have brought provides plenty of genuine new wants of a material kind, and if those fail, we always have our advertising industry to provide spurious ones. I do not think the

social dividend would be likely to turn us into a nation of laya-
bouts, or harm the drive to make Britain competitive.

Professor Dore's illuminating discussions of the work of humanity
and the problem of maintaining work incentive are highly germane to
our essay problem. But his method of distributing shares may amount
to confiscation of present ownership, since the companies are required
to issue new shares without receiving anything in return. Compare this
to the Kitty Hawk USOP, in which the companies get their capital
additions paid for by issuing USOP shares.

Professor Dore would reply to the charge of confiscation that any
measure that results, over time, in some people having fewer rights
to property income and other people having more, constitutes a confiscation of the property of the people who lose. The trick is to do it
in such a way that the pain attending the loss is minimized. Professor
Dore believes that both his plan and the Kitty Hawk plan "diminish
the pain as compared with requiring people to sit down and write out
a cheque returning to the state money which they have once received—as a capital levy does, for example."

Finally, the Social Democratic Party's Working Party on Share
Ownership recently published some plans they deem worthy of further
study. In SDP Open Forum No. 11, entitled "Wider Share Ownership—Equality and Opportunity in An Enterprise Economy" they summarize existing profit-sharing and employee share ownership plans in
Great Britain, and go on to recommend serious consideration of plans
for "citizens' ownership," as distinguished from profit-sharing and
employee ownership. They outline a citizens' unit trust, under which
every productive enterprise over a certain size (e.g., profits of £1
million) would contribute a share of profits each year to buy its own
shares for the trust. This would be tax-deductible so that it would
amount to a 2 1/2 percent rise in corporation tax. Over twenty years,
a stake of 10 percent would be built up in all major enterprises in the
country, regardless of whether they were companies, partnerships, or
cooperatives. Ownership of the shares would be elective, and individual citizens would effectively be life tenants, so that there is no need
to create a share-for-a-share register. (This would seem to make it
similar to the Perry National Dividend Plan, where the beneficiaries
are not really shareholders but just receive a share of the profits from
a part of the corporate income tax.)

The SDP Working Party goes on to say that a 10 percent interest
in quoted British companies would produce about £25 per head per
annum. Adding about £50 billion worth of state assets, which would

also go into the trust, might conribute another £50 per head per annum. If distributed among all citizens and if it included the unquoted private sector, the annual dividend per person after twenty years, would be £200 to £300 per household of two adults. These would be nonvoting shares, and would not be saleable, because of the belief that the poor would soon liquidate their shares. Further details of the SDP Working Party's studies will be found in Appendix D.

The Working Party raises the question of whether "all the palaver of setting up this trust and distributing shares to customers is worth it to provide income of about £200 per two-adult household." They conclude that it is worthwhile as a start toward citizens' ownership. This dramatizes the importance of selecting the ideal reservoir for share distribution, which we discussed in Section 3f above. In my opinion, only a deep reservoir comparable to the $300 billion annual capital additions of the Kitty Hawk model makes the game worth the palaver. Again, my knowledge of British finance is not up to the task of making exact projections, and I shall leave that to you essayists. There is, however, one published estimate that you can use as a starting point. William Norris, former Parliamentary Correspondent (and now an American Correspondent) for *The London Times*, made the estimate in his article, "SuperStock," published in the Autumn 1984 issue of *City Periscope*. He assumed that £24 billion worth of new capital would be added annually to British businesses, and that ownership of this capital would be shared equally by all Britons. He concluded:

> This would give around £400 of capital investment to every man, woman and child in the country. Say, £1,600 per family. Over 20 years, assuming no growth, each family would own capital worth £32,000, and an investment income of about £3,200.

Apparently Mr. Norris's estimate assumed a 10 percent annual pretax return on invested capital, and that total annual investment in new capital would not increase beyond today's £24 billion figure.

Thus, use of the new capital reservoir could produce £3,200 per year in capitalist income, as against a few hundred pounds per year through the schemes discussed in SDP Open Forum No. 11. Any attempts to stretch those schemes quickly approach the level of confiscation. Shallow reservoirs such as corporate profits, corporate income taxes, and outright capital dilution of present ownership are likely to produce shallow results. Why not let USOP draw upon the deepest reservoir of capitalism? Or, to put it another way, why not hook up USOP to the engine of capitalism, rather than trying to run on the exhaust fumes?

11.

TESTING AND SAFEGUARDING USOP

Obviously, the adoption of USOP would cause sweeping economic and social changes. We could guard against unwanted side effects, such as inflation and erosion of the work incentive, by installing USOP gradually. The Kitty Hawk model has this built-in safeguard because it is by nature a gradual plan that would take 20 years or more to come to full fruition. Perhaps the enabling legislation for USOP should call for an annual review of its progress and side effects by a legislative committee or a national commission.

Beyond gradualism, can we devise a test program that will give us a clear advance indication of the probable operating effects of USOP? Senator Mike Gravel (Democrat of Alaska) tackled that problem in 1977, when he was a member of the U.S. Senate Finance Committee. He had picked up the USOP concept from the 1976 Joint Economic Committee Report and had put his staff to work on a test program that he could propose in legislation. He called his scheme the "Full-Return Stock Plan" because of the requirement that all earnings must be distributed to shareholders as dividends. He proposed a small-scale test of the plan, selecting 40,000 test shareholders a year for five years, for a total of 200,000 shareholders in the test group. The shareholders were to be chosen at random from all 50 states, and from four groups: the blind and disabled, the low-income working poor, middle-income taxpayers, and Social Security recipients. At the end of the five-year period, each shareholder would own $20,000 worth of shares.

Unfortunately, before Senator Gravel could get his Full-Return Stock Plan into legislation, he was defeated in the 1980 Democratic Primary. My opinion is that his test program, while a step in the right direction, would not be likely to produce conclusive evidence of USOP's desirability because the test was too small to discern major consequences of the plan. I believe that a larger-scale test is in order, if we are to have any test program. It can be argued that the Kitty Hawk model is itself a test program, since it gradually democratizes access to long-term credit over the span of a generation. However, for those who insist upon a more segmented test plan, there are other possibilities. These include the use of public utilities as a test bed; the use of mergers, acquisitions, and takeovers; and the use of privatized government-owned facilities and services.

Ishier Jacobson, president and chief executive officer of Citizens' Utilities Company, one of America's most consistently profitable privately owned utilities, has suggested that the regulated utilities would be an ideal test bed for USOP, because shareholders of regulated public utilities do not gain any leverage from debt financing. The earnings fixed by utility regulators consist of a specified percentage return on the *equity* component of the utility's capital, and only the interest and issuance cost amortization is allowed on the debt. Therefore, if utilities were required to pay for their new capital additions by issuance of USOP shares instead of using retained earnings and debt, they would be less affected than would non-utility companies. Mr. Jacobson points out that the debt portion of utility capital is usually between 50 and 65 percent of the total capital of the utility, and that regulated utilities account for about 25 percent of the annual new capital expenditures in the United States. Accordingly, if we used the public utilities as a USOP test bed, we could get a nationwide test that would encompass annual capital expenditures of about $75 billion (25 percent of the $300 billion-dollar annual total reservoir), and for the most part, we would be replacing utility debt that brings no return to the present shareholders of the utilities.

As to mergers, acquisitions, and takeovers, we have previously noted that the present expenditure is about $124 billion per year in the United States, much of this in the form of debt, some of which is questionable enough to be branded "junk bonds." This area could also be used as a test bed, and if coupled with the $75 billion annual public utility expenditure, it would bring the test program to a healthy total of about $200 billion a year in new capital or takeover expenditures.

Finally, the nationalized companies in the United Kingdom, and the candidates for privatization of federal services in the United States, could also function as test beds. An excellent reference on this point is *Privatizing Federal Spending: A Strategy to Eliminate the Deficit*, by Stuart M. Butler. Mr. Butler makes a fascinating case for privatization of Amtrak, the National Passenger Railroad System; public lands; the postal service; and other government services and facilities.

Beyond these test programs, we should also think about building safeguards and backstops into the permanent USOP program, so that if conditions change, or if unforeseen problems crop up during its implementation, we are not stuck with a faulty plan or with damaging elements of an otherwise useful plan. Again, I believe that the gradual nature of the Kitty Hawk model takes care of some of this, but you may well wish to address this problem more specifically and try to erect your own safeguards and backstops.

12.

USOP AT THE LOCAL LEVEL

As we saw above in Section 3e, there is room for differences of opinion as to whether USOP shares should carry voting power. One solution, suggested by Ward Morehouse, president of the Council on International and Public Affairs, is to establish a Federal USOP board of directors, who would nominate USOP directors to the boards of participating companies. They could also oversee the issuance of USOP shares, acting as liaison among companies, banks, and government, and they could supervise the distribution of dividends to the USOP fund and from there to the USOP shareholders.

Mr. Morehouse also suggests that the members of the Federal USOP board be selected by the USOP board of the state which they represent. The following description of state and local versions of USOP is based on Mr. Morehouse's writings.

Each state would establish a USOP Board, with its members directly elected for staggered six-year terms by universal franchise. Their functions, in addition to selecting the member of the Federal USOP Board to represent their state, would be essentially the same as the Federal USOP Board. They would have responsibility for determining which companies within a given state were eligible to participate in that state's USOP, following criteria established at the national level by the Federal USOP Board but with some reasonable scope for variation at the state level to be responsive to particular circumstances in a given state.

Under a three-tiered USOP approach to universal capitalism, local communities would also be empowered to create their own USOPs at the municipal or county levels. Each local USOP board would be composed of people from that community, directly elected by universal franchise, somewhat on the principle of Representative Town Meetings in New England towns which have grown too large to let the entire population participate directly. State USOP Boards would establish an overall policy framework for local USOPs, in much the same manner as state legislatures now define the scope and powers of municipal governments.

The functions of local USOP boards would be broadly the same as the state or federal boards but they would be subject to some supervision by state boards to assure that they were following overall state policies, and that enterprises joining the local USOP met appropriate criteria which would give reasonable assurance for the financial soundness of the local USOP.

Local USOP boards might wish to experiment with the "stakeholder concept" —i.e., assuring that there would be representation, possibly weighted, of all those categories of people having a significant stake in a particular enterprise: workers, managers, existing owners, consumers, and the community at large. For example, workers and managers/owners have a larger direct stake in their own enterprise than do consumers and the community at large, so that they might be given a proportionately stronger voice in the operation of the enterprise. Combinations of USOPs and ESOPs are also possible so that workers could acquire some direct equity in an enterprise, in addition to that which would be held indirectly for them, as members of the community, through the local USOP.

Mr. Morehouse believes that state and local USOPs would be particularly relevant to the task of community economic revitalization, by providing access to capital for already established enterprises serving the community—the best single source for new jobs. He also sees an important interplay between state and local USOPs and the "enterprise zone" concept.

Enterprise zones seek to provide a basket of incentives to encourage the generation of jobs within designated geographical areas subject to chronically high unemployment. While the incentives vary, the most substantial usually involve exemption from, or reduction of, taxes over a period of time until the facility being created or expanded is well established.

What enterprise zones do not do, by and large, is to provide access to capital on attractive terms. The result is that only well-established businesses which have already accumulated substantial capital internally or have such well-established credit that they can secure capital on reasonable terms, are able to take advantage of the incentives offered. By contrast, USOPs would provide access to capital—in the form of equity rather than debt—on favorable terms.

If a USOP were combined with an enterprise zone—or if a business activity were to expand in an enterprise zone within a broader area being served by a USOP—the combination of incentives should provide a powerful inducement to the creation of new jobs within depressed communities, thus accelerating their economic revitalization.

Mr. Morehouse's three-tier concept gives USOP an exciting new dimension. It could also bring citizens more closely into contact with the USOP system and make them feel more a part of it through state and local participation. In that sense, it would truly democratize capitalism.

The Morehouse concept also provides a provocative challenge to essayists to tackle the difficult job of relating the macroeconomic USOP to the state and local levels. There are obvious advantages to such a three-tiered USOP model. Questions that you might address are whether this would unduly bureaucratize the USOP scheme; whether it can be carried to the state and local levels without losing the financial stability of using the most successful companies as the reservoir for diffusion of capital ownership; and whether the building of the state and local tiers should await the implementation of the federal USOP model.

13.

INTERNATIONAL AND THIRD-WORLD ASPECTS OF USOP

Some of the third-world and international aspects of USOP were explored in my 1984 book, *How to End the Nuclear Nightmare*. There I suggested that adoption of USOP by the United States would remove the ideological basis for enmity between the United States and the Soviet Union, since it would remove the exploitation factor from American capitalism and thereby remove the reason for class struggle. In connection with that book, the Council on International and Public Affairs sponsored a 1985 essay contest on the topic, "How can we, without adopting socialism or giving up our treasured freedoms, modify American capitalism to make it more equitable and reduce the level of ideological conflict with the Soviet Union so as to make possible an end to the nuclear nightmare?" Many excellent essays were written on this topic, and they are still coming in at this writing.

Since there is no point in duplicating those essays in the present competition, I do not suggest that you write on that international aspect of USOP. You might, however, consider writing about how adoption of USOP would affect the foreign policies of the United States and the United Kingdom toward Europe and NATO, Latin America, and the Third World in general—provided you believe that ideology actually affects foreign policies and relations among nations. There are many who believe that ideology is irrelevant, or is not a significant factor in such relations.

The present essay contest concentrates on the mechanics of USOP

126

structures. In that connection, you might want to speculate on how the USOP concept might be used within developing nations. USOP, of course, is designed for industrialized nations whose large business enterprises furnish a ready foundation for broadening MOP ownership through capital expansion, credit power, and ability to make self-liquidating capital additions. But what about the developing nations, a category that includes most countries and most of the earth's population? (These nations are also called nonindustrialized, underdeveloped, Third World, or just plain poor.) What they are trying to develop is a higher standard of living, and almost invariably they see industrialization as the quickest way to that end.

Even now, the industrial countries are deeply involved in helping developing nations to industrialize. These efforts involve three forms of financing: foreign capital in the form of loans or equity investments, foreign-aid handouts, and capital investments made in conjunction with wealthy local financiers or businesses. In all three cases, little or no new capital ownership is created among the local residents, most of whom were poor before such aid and remain poor afterwards. Therefore, this financing, even in the form of handouts, is generally not much appreciated by most local residents. In fact, their resentment often results in the expropriation of foreign investments. Moreover, the few jobs created by these efforts usually do not significantly increase the purchasing power of developing nations. To reach that goal, industrialization combined with the diffusion of capital ownership would appear the best approach. This opens the way for the United States and Great Britain to improve relations with developing nations by helping them to install their own USOP system.

Obviously, Third World implementation of USOP would not be easy, but there is at least one potentially viable scenario. Suppose that American or British multinational corporations were able to secure the necessary guarantees of credit through the World Bank. This would enable them to establish industrial enterprises that would eventually be owned by the local citizens once the USOP shares had paid for themselves out of earnings. The multinationals could supply the management and the technology. At the same time, they would be taking advantage of lower costs of raw material and labor, which might result in higher profits and quicker repayment of capital investments. That has, in fact, always been one of the big attractions of the Third World for the multinationals.

This use of USOP, if viable, would improve our relations with many foreign countries and make us much more popular in the United Nations General Assembly. It would also create new customers for

American and British business. Local industries would be able to pay the multinationals for their goods and services, and the local residents, with more cash in their pockets from capital ownership, might become customers for imported goods and services. How such a plan could be implemented in specific Third World countries would require detailed study, of course, but it appears to have a much better chance for success than any of the strategies currently employed by the State Department and our multinationals. And it could enable Third World nations to build enterprises that would ultimately be owned directly and individually by needy citizens, rather than corrupt government officials or a few wealthy locals who bank the profits abroad.

Franklin R. Stewart, director of the Center for Study of Expanded Capital Ownership in Washington, D.C. is a former U.S. State Department official who has spent much of his life assisting developing nations. He believes that the USOP concept has a broad application to the Third World. In association with Professor Edward E. Azar, director of the Center for International Development at the University of Maryland, he has been exploring the possibilities of converting some portion of the external debt of Third-World nations to equity, with that equity to be widely owned by the people of those countries. Their acquisition of the equity could be financed through some form of democratization of credit, such as USOP. This would make a valuable essay topic, as would privatization of state-owned or state-controlled enterprises in the Third World through a modified version of USOP.

Professor Azar has published two important papers that should be consulted by essayists who address the Third-World aspects of USOP: "Development Diplomacy," and "U.S. Comprehensive Regional Policy for the Middle East" (see Bibliography Section). In "Development Diplomacy," Professor Azar demonstrates the importance of adding a new dimension to our relations with Third-World nations:

> There are several ways of describing, discovering, and explaining sources of conflict in the Third World as a whole and in the Near East in particular. But underlying all descriptions are three common points. First, conflict situations caused by inequalities built into the social systems of the countries concerned tend to be protracted. Second, they divert the world's time and resources, as well as those of the unstable country itself, and reduce the ability and will of capable or interested actors to "solve" them. And, finally these conflicts tend to defy the unilateral or multilateral management skills applied to them....

I suggest that the core goal of any meaningful development plan must be to reduce inequality. Not only does growth of the economic sector without reduction of inequality seem morally lacking, but I would argue that it will also be doomed to failure as the economic system becomes hyperdeveloped and is no longer organically related to the rest of the social organization....

Because no sustained economic growth can occur unless it is accompanied by reorganization of the rest of the social system with which the economy is interdependent, development policies focusing solely on economic development are doomed to fail. Thus, we need to focus on interdependencies in social structure when designing development plans. [pp. 138-42]

Professor Azar sees universal local ownership as a means of reducing inequality within Third World nations. Therefore, he recommends intensive study of USOP as a potentially valuable element of our Third-World policy. To that end, he has sponsored seminar and workshop discussions of USOP at the University of Maryland.

14.

NOMENCLATURE

One of the most difficult tasks associated with a plan of this type is finding the right name. At one time, I called it *SuperStock*. Some people found that name very apt but others thought it was too gimmicky and might trivialize the concept. Some think that *Universal Capitalism* is the most appropriate name since it is the most basic description of the plan, but others feel it is too ponderous a title. Some think a more dramatic title such as *The Third Way* would be appropriate. Britain's Social Democratic Party has coined the term *Citizen's Ownership*. After ten years, the best I have been able to come up with is USOP—Universal Share Ownership Plan. Perhaps with a fresh eye you can do better. USOP was suggested by my son, James J. Speiser, who feels that it is a complete description of the plan, and also that it ties the plan to the well-established ESOP. He also believes that the first two letters of USOP will be read as "us" by millions of people who have always perceived capitalists as "them."

The certificates that evidence USOP share ownership should also have a name. They could be called simply "USOP shares," the term I have used in this book. But if it turns out that we do not use common shares and that we undertake to create an entirely new concept of ownership for USOP, then we probably should have a new name, such as *Capital Ownership Certificate*. Professor James Meade, as part of his plan for a social dividend, uses the term *National Capital Fund Share Certificate*. Can you come up with anything better for the USOP certificate?

15.

NEXT STEPS

Clearly, we need to focus our best minds and strongest resources on the implementation of USOP, for it has centuries of inertia to overcome, and it must carry the heaviest of all burdens: It sounds too good to be true. To become a political issue and eventually be enacted into law, USOP needs to be analyzed and debated in universities, religious groups, the media, political circles, and finally, the legislatures. Here is a fertile field for those of you adept at organization and communication. What next steps should be taken to put USOP into the center of public debate, in time for the political campaigns of 1987-88 on both sides of the Atlantic?

The present essay contests themselves are, in a sense, the next step for USOP. Assuming that there are lots of good essays submitted and that these are published, along with appropriate commentary—what should we do to carry on the idea from there?

Should there be a federal commission established by Congress (or a Royal Commission in Britain) to study USOP? Should one or more universities organize a mock USOP commission to simulate the work of a government commission? Or should we bypass the commission format in favor of direct action by Congress and Parliament?

What should we do to build support for USOP in the business and financial communities? Will mention of the universal ownership principle in the second draft of the American Catholic Bishops' pastoral (No. 288) spur debate in the religious community? And are there any national organizations that might undertake promotion of USOP, or should a new organization be created for that purpose? (A small start has been made by formation of the Center for Study of Expanded Capital Ownership, 1216 16th Street, N.W., Washington, D.C. 20036.)

If your talents run to political science, you might take a crack at drafting the legislation needed to implement USOP. This is not a simple task, because many complicated tax and banking laws will be encountered in the process of carving out a niche for USOP. It would be very valuable to have such draft legislation laid out, so that legislators considering the concept can have a more concrete idea of just what changes would be required.

Some of the important clauses to consider are those relating to determination of which companies would participate in USOP; the requirement of full payout of earnings to shareholders; the elimination or modification of the corporate income tax; eligibility and priorities for becoming USOP shareholders; role of the banks in providing the loans required to pay for USOP shares initially, and the interest provisions relating to those loans; methods of keeping the interest rate on USOP share loans at the lowest possible level through government guarantees; organization and management of the USOP trust fund, which would hold the shares and pay out the dividends; organization of the federal USOP board, and possibly state and local USOP boards as well; and methods of speeding up income to USOP shareholders, such as dividing dividends between repayment of loan interest and principal and direct income to USOP shareholders.

APPENDIX A

CENTER FOR STUDY OF EXPANDED CAPITAL OWNERSHIP

1216 16th Street, N.W.
Washington, DC 20036
(202) 223-8501

Franklin R. Stewart
Director

Robert D. Hamrin
Chief Economist

THE ECONOMIC FEASIBILITY OF
EXPANDED CAPITAL OWNERSHIP

A Note on the Seminar on
Policies for Capital Diffusion
through Expanded Equity Ownership
Brookings Institution
Washington, D.C.
December 30, 1977

The Seminar was organized by Senator Mike Gravel (Alaska), a member of the Senate Finance Committee, and was chaired by Professor Lawrence R. Klein of the Wharton School of Finance at the University of Pennsylvania. The purpose of the Seminar was to determine the economic feasibility of greatly expanded capital ownership through government guaranteed loans. The basic conclusion was that such a plan could be made workable and was not inherently inflationary.

133

*Seminar on Policies for Capital Diffusion
through Expanded Equity Ownership*

Brookings Institution
Washington, D.C.
September 30, 1977

Participating in the day-long Seminar held at the Brookings Institution were a number of leading professional economists, as well as senior officials from government and business. The Seminar was designed to assist Senator Gravel in drafting legislation to test a stock distribution plan that closely resembles the SuperStock plan later proposed by Stuart M. Speiser. Senator Gravel called his concept the *Full Return Stock Plan*, the name being based on the feature which would require corporations to pay out as dividends the entire earnings (full return) of a special class of stock.

In broad outline, Senator Gravel's plan reads as follows:

> I propose a new approach to capital expansion which would diffuse ownership of new capital to those who have not previously reaped the benefits of capital ownership. In simple outline the plan would guarantee private loans to purchase corporate stock, with the new capital being used by the corporation to pay for the expansion of plant and equipment. The stock would be held as security for the loan, and dividends used for repayment. After the loan is fully or partially retired, the investor would receive dividend income. The plan provides investment capital for industry while developing an alternate source of income for those who historically have depended on their labor income alone. The plan would not transfer existing wealth from the rich to the poor, but rather allow the poor to obtain a share of the new wealth generated by our capital expansion.
>
> The plan should be tested on a limited scale to determine its effect on individuals, corporations, government and the economy as a whole. In each of five consecutive years $800 million in private, federally guaranteed loans could be made available to participants in amounts of $20,000 per family unit...the test program would involve about 40,000 participants per year for five years for a total of 200,000 participants. This would give a sufficiently large and representative sample for analytical purposes....
>
> The proposal contemplates the creation of a new class of corporate stock. The stock, referred to as Full Return Stock, would be preferred as to dividends and have its share of corporate earnings distributed quarterly....

Participants would be drawn from a cross section of American society. They would be chosen at random from four target groups: the blind and disabled, low income working poor, middle income taxpayers, and Social Security recipients.

There was a spirited and detailed discussion of the plan, considering its effects on the economy as a whole, on the securities markets, on inflation, and on individual households. No minutes were taken, but the written comments of the moderator, Professor Lawrence Klein, covered all the major questions raised about feasibility of the plan. On the aspect of the plan that would require expansion of the money supply to provide credit for the stock purchases, Professor Klein concluded that "the expansion of Federal Reserve credit will not be inflationary if the funds made available flow into investment that raises national productivity."

As to the effect of the plan on household savings decisions, Professor Klein stated:

> If households have their regular income expectations from normal growth of wages and then augment this by expected future earnings from equity holdings (with full earnings pay-out), they will probably raise their savings to agree with the higher discounted stream of future (expected) receipts. They will not have to consume less if the scheme stimulates investment and shifts the growth path of income to a higher level through a regular multiplier process.

As to the effect on the corporations whose stock is distributed under the plan, Professor Klein stated:

> In many cases, it may be expected that the additional investment made possible by the acquisition of Plan funds by business will increase the productivity of existing capital or capital acquired contemporaneously outside the Plan. As investment is enhanced throughout the whole economy, firms generally will benefit from the induced increase in total output.

Based on the generally favorable discussion at the Seminar, and the absence of any findings that the plan could not be made workable, Senator Gravel issued a detailed report in December 1977 which incorporated into a new draft the results of the Brookings Seminar discussions. The basic structure of his *Full Return Stock Plan* remained intact, with several refinements suggested by the conclusions reached at the Seminar.

APPENDIX B

The following four articles constitute the symposium on the broadening of capital ownership published in the *Journal of Post Keynesian Economics*, VII, No. 3 (Spring 1985), pages 422-442. They are reprinted here with permission of the publisher, M.E. Sharpe, Inc. Armonk, New York 10504.

The term "SuperStock" in these articles refers to the Kitty Hawk model of USOP.

Can effective demand and the movement toward further income equality be maintained in the face of robotics? An introduction

PAUL DAVIDSON

The author is Professor of Economics at Rutgers University.

In her *Essays in the Theory of Economic Growth* Joan Robinson analyzed "A Model for the Future" (1963, pp. 17-21). In this 1963 vision of a futuristic capitalistic economy, where the industrial sector is manned mainly by robots while most "workers" are employed in the service sector, severe difficulties can develop in either maintaining effective demand levels sufficiently to absorb the full employment output and/or in preventing "workers" in the service sector from suffering a severe fall in real income.

> ...how easy it is, in this [robotic] model, for the economy to be let down by its bootstraps....The queer appearance of this model is due to the fact that it represents an economy in which conventions and rules are being observed after they have ceased to be appropriate to the technical situation. (Robinson, 1963, p. 21)

Recent trends in the United States suggest that Robinson's future may already be upon us. In the recovery phase of recent business cycles, the improvement in real income has not been matched by a recovery in employment sufficient to reduce unemployment rates relative to the rate observed in the previous upper turning point of the business cycle, as the use of robots rapidly displaces workers in the industrial sector. More ominously, the size of the population below the poverty line has increased in recent years despite the surge in business activity since 1982.

Have the results of Joan Robinson's vision of a robotic economy come home to roost? And if so what changes in conventions and rules can be adopted that are more appropriate to the existing new technologies and that will improve the operations of the real economy?

In the following pages, Stuart Speiser, an eminent lawyer, suggests a scheme for altering the rules and conventions for acquiring ownership of the means of production in order to spread the income generating capacity of capital among the members of an economy (*without* requiring state ownership of the capital stock and centralized investment project decision-making). Speiser's scheme, which he calls SuperStock, is exceedingly simple—and perhaps, in the eyes of some,

even naive. Nevertheless there is nothing in the scheme which necessarily involves a *real* resource constraint. In other words, the scheme
is economically feasible. What is involved is a significant change in
the legal and financial rules for acquiring property rights in the major
private corporate entities which will continue to make the significant
decisions regarding production flows and real capital accumulation.

Moreover, the Speiser scheme squarely faces the unresolved question of Keynes's revolution, namely, the "arbitrary and inequitable
distribution of wealth and income" (Keynes, 1936, p. 372). The Roosevelt New Deal and the Kennedy-Johnson Fair Deal attempted to
improve the unemployment problem and simultaneously and painlessly
create a less arbitrary and inequitable distribution of income under the
protection of rapid economic growth where there were no real losers.
With the stagnation of the late 1960s and 1970s, however, programs
promoting a more equitable income distribution became less popular
in the United States as they foisted onto the middle and upper income
classes the pain of redistribution without the growth of real income.

In the 1980s, this pain of the potential losers of real income
culminated in the political popularity of programs to reverse the gains
in equality made in the past half century and to reestablish a more
structured inequality. The danger in this is that a "them vs. us" class
structure mentality may develop and may result in internal economic
and political dissension and conflict. Such unrest can undermine the
capitalist system—a system which when it operates in a manner in
which its fruits are widely and fairly dispersed has provided the best
means for achieving economic progress.

Speiser's SuperStock scheme is one suggestion for ameliorating
these potential problems while maintaining the capitalist system's inherent advantages of decentralized decision making and the play of
self-interest (cf. Keynes, 1936, p. 380). It has as its objective the widest
possible spreading of the fruits of capitalism's progress while maintaining high levels of effective demand via private decision making.

The SuperStock scheme will obviously have some implications
for organized security markets—just as the then unconventional government backed VA and FHA mortgage scheme had important implications for money markets after the Second World War. Yet as long
as SuperStock is limited to the top 1,000 or 2,000 corporations, organized security markets can still have the casino aspect which some
find so advantageous. Those savers who like to play with casino-type
portfolios can still help finance "venture capitalist" firms, who by
their very nature and size would not come under the SuperStock proposal. If anything, Superstock, by reducing the use of ownership rights

in the top corporations as an important means for reaping capital gains, would encourage the financing of more venturesome projects by the more venturesome "savers."

The SuperStock proposal, even if it could perform as Speiser suggests is, of course, not a magic bullet to resolve all the perceived flaws of our current economic system. The SuperStock proposal would not address the problem of democracy in the workplace; nor would it, I believe, necessarily resolve the inflation problem. Nevertheless, it is just such unconventional suggestions which can act as the burr to stimulate innovative ideas in a dialogue on our existing income distribution problem—rather than leaving it to the (wishful?) belief that whatever economic growth results from a laissez-faire government role will, in the long run, resolve the problem of the inequitable distribution of income.

Recently some eminent economists (e.g., Meade, 1984; Brittan, 1984; Weitzman, 1984) have been turning their attention to devising schemes for broadening capital ownership and/or spreading the distribution of capital's income as a means of saving Western capitalist economies in the age of robotics. The SuperStock scheme is more unconventional than most; nevertheless, I believe, it is a most ingenious and well-developed plan, which safeguards our system of personal liberties. It deserves public discussion.

REFERENCES

Brittan, S. *The Role and Limits of Government*. London: Temple Smith, 1984.

Keynes, J. M. *The General Theory of Employment, Interest and Money*. New York: Harcourt, Brace, 1936.

Robinson, J. *Essays in The Theory of Economic Growth*. London: Macmillan, 1963.

Meade, J. "Full Employment, New Technologies and the Distribution of Income." *Journal of Social Policy*, April 1984, 13, Part 2.

Weitzman, M. L. *The Share Economy: Conquering Stagflation*. Cambridge, Mass.: Harvard University Press, 1984.

Broadened capital ownership—the solution to major domestic and international problems

STUART M. SPEISER

The author is a member of the bars of New York, Connecticut, and the District of Columbia.

Four major domestic and international problems that could be solved by making American capitalism universal are: (1) unemployment and the bleak outlook for job creation in the age of advanced robots and computers;
(2) the unfairness of American ·capitalism;
(3) the dilemma of liberation theology; and (4) the nuclear nightmare.[1]

In the present paper, only the first two problems, unemployment and unfairness, are treated.

American welfare capitalism: a system at war with itself

At the heart of American welfare capitalism is the concept of redistribution of income through transfer payments. Those of us who are fortunate enough to be productive—who have a job or own a profitable business—pay taxes to provide the money for transfer payments to keep a lot of less fortunate Americans from starving or revolting, or both. But this system of welfare (or mixed) capitalism is a relatively new one, and there is no proof that it can sustain itself on a long-term basis. In fact, mounting evidence both here and abroad indicates that the welfare state based on transfer payments is inherently inflationary, and thus potentially self-destructive.

The split society that results from the confrontation between capital and labor, haves and have-nots, owners and non-owners, is a persistent underlying problem. Government efforts to bridge the gap date back to FDR's New Deal, but they have never produced any substantial redistribution of wealth. The success of the trickle down theory depends largely upon its ability to create jobs, and that ability is rapidly disappearing. We now expect inflation rates of 10 percent or more whenever government intervenes to create employment. And neither political party has been able to find a way of reducing inflation other than by intentionally creating recession and unemployment.

Practically all traditional American economists look upon wealth and capital ownership as a permanent part of the social structure, rather than as a potential tool for income distribution. The time has come to face up to the ownership question—for in ownership of the means of production, we may find a solution to our own internal economic crises.

The four means of support

Americans obtain their financial support in four ways: by working for it (wages, salaries), by receiving government checks or charity (welfare, Social Security), by cheating (crime, tax evasion, welfare fraud, etc.), and by receiving a return on productive capital (capitalist income). The first three methods have been used throughout the world for centuries and have often been fostered by government policies. The fourth, return on capital, has never been used as a method of creating an equitable distribution of income. It has remained the sole province of the rich—the "capitalists" who have the savings or credit to buy corporate stock and other forms of income-producing capital.

Wages would be the ideal method of supporting people, but chronically high unemployment and increasing technological displacement indicate that no government—conservative or liberal—can create enough jobs to support everyone through wages. Furthermore, the age of robots is nearly upon us. The robot—the "steel-collar" worker—can work at peak efficiency 24 hours a day, 7 days a week without getting bored, at an hourly cost of no more than one-third the wages of the human being it replaces. Yet our great thinkers seem to be unaware of a monumental question: *Who will own the robots?*

SuperStock: The next step for capitalism

Wages, welfare, and cheating are used by virtually all economic systems. Only the return on capital is unique to capitalism. Capitalism has survived in the United States and other democracies because it can change. It can be an evolutionary system, flexible enough to keep up with the great sea of changes of history. When it started to come apart during the Great Depression, Franklin Roosevelt injected enough welfare socialism to stave off a revolution. But the anesthetic effect of the welfare injection is wearing off, and there's nothing left to save capitalism except capitalism itself.

Is there anything inherent in capitalism that would prevent us from spreading ownership of the means of production (MOP) to all of our people? You will search in vain for any such restriction in the Constitution or laws of the United States. Yet most economists, even liberals, have not opened their minds to such a concept. But there is no reason why capitalism cannot function when the means of production is owned by the majority of individuals rather than a minority. In fact, common sense and experience tell us that capitalism would probably work much better (especially in a democracy) if MOP ownership were in the hands of the largest possible group. If we could find a way to open MOP ownership to all Americans, we could make our economic system consistent with our political democracy and our concept of fairness.

There *is* a plan to make capitalism work for everyone. I call this plan SuperStock because it uses corporate stock to perform economic functions heretofore assigned to wages, welfare, and prayer. SuperStock is merely a working title, however. You may prefer a more conventional name, such as universal capitalism, democratic capitalism, social capitalism, new capitalism, or real capitalism.

I propose SuperStock as a potential means of solving many of our economic problems in a way that can also defuse the global conflict between capitalism and communism. But I do not claim it is the ultimate plan. Probably it is no more than the Wright brothers' model of universal capitalism. I present SuperStock as a starting point for discussion, to stimulate the study and debate that will lead to development of a Concorde model.

Our current corporate finance system—why the rich get richer

We generally define capital as all goods that are used in the production of other goods and services—the means of production. Today the main form of capital is the plant and equipment used by business; and in the United States, the main form of capital ownership is shares of stock in our major corporations.

There is a vast hidden reservoir of wealth in this country in the form of the *new capital* created each year by American business. This new capital is *self-liquidating*, meaning that it is designed to pay for itself out of the increased profits flowing from expanded production. What keeps most people from acquiring self-liquidating capital is lack of access to long-term credit.

In 1982, even at a time of crippling recession, American business invested over $300 billion in the construction and purchase of new plants and equipment. Under our present system, 95 percent of these new capital expenditures are paid for by a combination of debt (loans or bonds) and internal funds (retained earnings and investment tax credits). New equity in the form of newly issued stock sold in the market is responsible for only 5 percent of the financing.

The main vice of this system is that it perpetuates the overconcentration of capital ownership, since it creates no new capitalists. Even the 5 percent of capital expenditures that is paid for by the issuance of new stock can be owned only by those who have cash savings or credit. By definition, they are in the same pinnacle class as the present shareholders who automatically own the other 95 percent of new capital.

In addition to widening the wealth gap between owners and non-owners, this system keeps billions of dollars bottled up in the corporations for capital expenditures, thereby reducing the income available for mass consumption of the corporations' products. Wealthy stockholders believe this practice serves their interests, for they would otherwise have to pay income taxes on substantial dividend income. They prefer to have this money remain in corporate coffers where the value of their holdings can increase untaxed and without any additional investment on their part. There is nothing sacred about this system, however. It is simply one method—and not necessarily the best method—of financing an industrial economy.

How SuperStock would change this

SuperStock is designed to make stock in America's 2,000 leading corporations available through a change in this system that would funnel ownership of new capital directly to the 50 million households that own little or no capital. The object is to pipe the flow from the $300 billion new capital reservoir to the place where it is most needed: to the great majority of Americans (roughly 94 percent of the population) who have no substantial ownership now and who, under the present system, are highly unlikely ever to attain substantial capital ownership.

One way to do this would be to reduce the flow of internal funds and debt and make our major corporations pay for capital outlays by issuing new common stock. Then we could route all of this common stock into the hands of SuperStockholders—people who own no stock now and can't afford to buy any. But we don't have to make it a handout, for this stock has the unique ability to pay for itself. If we provided the SuperStockholders with the key ingredient that for centuries has enabled wealthy people to accumulate capital ownership—long-term credit—they could sit back and let this new stock pay for itself out of its own dividends.

Since corporations wouldn't be allowed to use internal funds for capital outlays, they would be able to pay out practically all of their earnings as dividends. We should also allow the corporations a tax deduction for the dividends paid on SuperStock shares, so that the SuperStockholders will benefit from the full pre-tax earnings. This should get the SuperStockholders' shares paid for in about 7 to 10 years, based on a pre-tax return of about 20 percent a year and allowing for a reasonable rate of interest.

Of course, the SuperStockholders couldn't qualify for credit to buy these shares, so the federal government would have to guarantee these loans, just as the FHA now guarantees mortgage loans. This could be done by the Treasury or by a new government agency, financed by loan insurance fees. The stock would remain in escrow until its dividends had paid for it; then it would be owned by the Super-Stockholders. Or, to speed the flow of income, half the dividends could be used for loan repayment and interest, and the other half could be paid directly to the SuperStockholders. To minimize the loan risks, and to make the earning power of our major corporations work for all Americans, we could give each SuperStockholder an identical diversified portfolio of all major corporations that make capital outlays.

The SuperStockholders would not be required to sign notes. The money would be owed by the SuperStock fund, and it would be secured by the assets and earning power of the 2,000 leading corporations that participate in the plan. In effect, the 50 million noncapitalist households would be using the credit power of our 2,000 major corporations to acquire shares of their stock, just as those corporations now use their credit power to acquire further capital ownership for their present stockholders, largely through the use of long-term credit. The plan also resembles the "leveraged buyout," which typically involves a few top executives of a large corporation who want to take over ownership for themselves, using the assets of the corporation as collateral for huge loans with which to buy out the present stockholders. Leveraged buyouts do not create jobs, spread ownership, raise profits, increase production, or improve management. Yet our major lenders have made billions of dollars available for such bootstrap financing. And few question the legitimacy of using the assets of major corporations to create hundreds of millions in profits out of mere paper transactions and to aggravate the existing overconcentration of capital ownership.

The changes made by SuperStock may seem radical, but they would not disturb present wealth, and they would not run afoul of any provisions of our Constitution or national policy, because we have no such provision relating to capital ownership.

The total privately owned productive capital in the United States is now about $5 trillion. Our corporations will probably be spending another $5 trillion on capital outlays within the next two decades. If we let ownership of this new capital flow to the SuperStockholders, the scales will be just about even. But if we use the old system, we'll just double the wealth of the pinnacle class, and leave 94 percent of Americans without any hope of becoming capitalists. We'll continue to deny them the main benefit of the capitalist system: ownership of productive capital.

Evening up the scales in this way could bring stock ownership of as much as $100,000 ($5 trillion divided by 50 million noncapitalist households) to practically every American household within one generation, with capitalist income of $10,000 to $20,000 per year. This would remove a major cause of social unrest and crime, and it would cause all Americans to root for higher profits. It would provide a massive infusion of purchasing power to match our huge productive capacity. It would help to reduce inflation by increasing production and by replacing welfare and Social Security payments with the return earned by productive capital. For the first time, we could become affluent enough to deal with problems like poverty, pollution, and health care.

The participating corporations would benefit by having a ready source of funds that are sorely needed for plant modernization, research and development, and other outlays designed to raise productivity and keep American industry competitive. They would also benefit from the elimination of their corporate income tax payments. This move would not be costly to the federal government. Currently, corporate taxes bring in less than 10 percent of federal revenue. Thanks to tax credits and loopholes, the average tax rate of our large corporations is only about 20 percent. Since all shareholders (including Super-Stockholders) would have to pay personal income taxes on the dividend income, the Treasury would probably collect more revenue than under the present system.

It would be up to Congress to determine the priorities and requirements for SuperStock ownership. We might start by excluding all households with current net worth of $100,000 or more. There is precedent for such government distribution. During the nineteenth century, when land was the main form of productive capital, the government distributed land to Americans through the Homestead Act, giving 160 acres to anyone who was willing to settle and cultivate it for five years.

Congress could consider a point system for eligibility. Points could be added for low wages, physical disability, lack of savings or capital ownership, willingness to work, compliance with the law, and public service work. Points could be deducted for criminal violations, capital ownership over a certain level, unwillingness to work, high wages, and so on. We might also consider giving special priority to the armed forces, police and fire departments, health-care workers, and perhaps even politicians—people engaged in demanding or dangerous public service that leaves them little opportunity to accumulate capital honestly. The idea is to make participation in SuperStock more attractive to public servants than bribery or featherbedding.

I believe that SuperStockholders should not be permitted to vote their shares or transfer them, except possibly by inheritance. SuperStock is not intended to change the control of corporations or to destroy the business skill that took us generations to develop. If SuperStock were voting stock, the voting power might be manipulated by special interest groups seeking control of our major corporations. Making SuperStock nontransferable would avoid the speculation and squandering that marred the Homestead Act and would assure that SuperStock would have no effect on the stockmarket trading of the participating corporations' present shares.

While these restrictions will deny the holders of SuperStock some of the advantages of earned or inherited wealth, the immediate reason for the plan is to heal our split society by using stock ownership to make income distribution more equitable. (An element of voting could be injected by allowing the SuperStockholders to elect a few directors of major corporations, or allowing them to elect the directors of the SuperStock fund, who in turn could elect some directors of the 2,000 participating corporations.)

Please note that SuperStock does not involve issuing shares of stock of a particular corporation to its employees. Employee ownership, while an attractive idea, offers no benefits to the unemployed, the very poor, or the great majority of Americans who cannot look forward to long-term jobs with our most prosperous companies. There is no way to plug our neediest people into the powerhouse of the American economy through worker or employee ownership—there are simply not enough jobs with those strong corporations to go around.

Some background on the SuperStock plan

SuperStock represents my modification of the long-standing ideas of other writers. In 1976, the basic idea was studied by the Joint Economic Committee of Congress, which issued a favorable report on it. The report included these recommendations:

Whatever the means used, the basic objective should be to distribute newly created capital broadly among the population. Such
a policy would redress a major imbalance in our society and has
the potential for strengthening future business growth. (1976, pp.
99-100)

In 1977, the concept was discussed by about thirty-five economists, financial experts, and government officials at an all-day Brookings Institution seminar. Most of those present agreed that the plan
was worth a test, and no one pointed out any reason why it could not
be made to work.

On September 12, 1984, Dr. David Owen, leader of the Social
Democratic Party of Great Britain, proposed to the party's annual
convention that they adopt a plan similar to SuperStock, under which
all British citizens would become shareholders of the nationalized
corporations, to be followed by share ownership in privately held
corporations.

Clearly, there is no theoretical or institutional obstacle to the
implementation of a plan like SuperStock. Most economists consider
income distribution to be a political question. We could readily adopt
SuperStock if the national will and consensus were behind it. No doubt
there would be unforeseen problems, but at least we would start out
with a system that is consistent with our political democracy and one
that is capable of eliminating the international class warfare that lies
at the root of nuclear confrontation.

As early as 1936, John Maynard Keynes realized that the problem
of equitable income distribution could not be solved by creating jobs
and that this task would have to be accomplished by socialization of
capital ownership. In his great work, *The General Theory of Employment, Interest and Money*, he concluded: "A somewhat comprehensive
socialization of investment will prove the only means of seeing an
approximation to full employment" (1936, p. 378). However, he did
not advocate state ownership of the means of production. In his later
years, he proposed distribution of stock to those who could not afford
to buy it. Clearly then, we need a plan like SuperStock to make capital
ownership fill the huge gaps caused by our inability to create enough
jobs and the inflationary effects of the welfare state.

Let no one dismiss SuperStock as utopian, for utopian ideas rest
on changes in human nature, while SuperStock accepts human nature
as it is and deals with the realities of the corporate finance system.

NOTES

[1]On the last point (see Speiser, 1984) I contend that if capital ownership

were opened to all Americans, this would remove the exploitation factor from American capitalism; and that having made the ideological conflict between capitalism and Marxism irrelevant, the United States would be in a better position to conduct meaninguful disarmament negotiations with the Soviet Union.

REFERENCES

Joint Economic Committee, 94th Congress, 2nd Session, *The 1976 Joint Economic Report*, Senate Report No. 94-690, pp. 99-100.

Keynes, J.M. *The General Theory of Employment, Interest and Money.* New York: Harcourt, Brace, 1936.

Speiser, S.M. *How to End The Nuclear Nightmare.* New York: North River Press/Dodd Mead, 1984.

Beyond SuperStock: the three-tiered plan for universal capital ownership

Ward Morehouse

The author is the president of the Council of International and Public Affairs and a Research Associate at Columbia University's School of International Affairs.

This article is adapted from a paper presented to The Other Economic Summit, London, June 6-10, 1984, entitled "Economic Justice in the Next Economy: Strategies for Universalizing Capital Ownership."

I have one fundamental difficulty with the SuperStock concept if it is to be confined to the 2,000 largest corporations in the United States. My reservation is both political and economic. The political concern stems from my conviction that there is already too great concentration of economic power in U.S. society, and, if providing government-guaranteed credit for new capital spending would only increase that concentration, I believe it would have deleterious consequences for society as a whole (although I do recognize Speiser's counter argument that, with equity ownership so broadly distributed, large corporations would perforce become much more conscious of and responsive to broader social and environmental needs and values).

The economic dimension is at least as compelling. If Paul Hawken (1984) and other popular critics of the existing economic paradigm in the United States are right in their analysis of the large-scale corporate sector, the very largest corporations—say, the *Fortune* list of the 1,000 largest industrial corporations in the United States—are moving into a period in which they are less likely to exercise such a dominant role in the U.S. economy. Hawken suggests that younger, smaller, more vibrant companies that are starting out with a more positive information/mass ratio in the goods and services they produce are likely to be a better bet over the longer term with respect to overall performance. I would therefore urge that SuperStock be broadened from the outset to include all companies with publicly traded stock and satisfactory earnings records. (Some screening process would be necessary to exclude, in the early stages until the SuperStock plan was established and the risk of failure widely distributed, shaky or marginal companies.)

With that qualification, however, I wholeheartedly support the SuperStock plan, not because I believe it is the last word in bringing about universal capital ownership in the United States. Rather, I think it is a highly plausible place to begin the kind of widespread public debate essential if we are going to realize the kind of fundamental shift in patterns of ownership of productive assets in the United States essential to bringing about a more equitable and just economic order.

In my view the SuperStock plan should be seen as the first leg or opening wedge in the restructuring of the American economic system to achieve such a social order. Other characteristics of the larger concept of social capitalism[1] such as greater self-governance through user ownership of housing and community facilities and more democratic local ownership and control of the means of producing goods and services will require something more.

In contrast to an employee stock ownership plan or ESOP, SuperStock is a general stock ownership plan or GSOP. The distinction, of course, is that in the former only employees of a particular enterprise get a piece of the action while in the latter everyone within a given jurisdiction does, at least as a matter of principle. GSOPs have been briefly on the statute books in the United States (under legislation introduced at the instance of the then-Senator from Alaska Mike Gravel, who was seeking a vehicle for sharing with all of the citizens of the State of Alaska dividends from the Alaskan oil pipeline). Unfortunately, that GSOP legislation was lacking some crucial ingredients, including government guarantee of credit for acquisition of productive assets and incentives for enterprises to become a part of GSOP such as relief from the corporate income tax. Nonetheless, the basic concept was seen as sufficiently plausible for it to be enacted into law.

In an effort to determine the feasibility of GSOPs from the point of view of mainstream academic and business economists, a Seminar on Policies for Capital Diffusion through Expanded Equity Ownership was held at the Brookings Institution in September 1977. The general conclusion, as set forth by Professor Lawrence Klein of the University of Pennsylvania, moderator of the seminar, was that there was no economic reason why the plan could not be made workable and that—on one potentially troublesome point of whether it would be inflationary—the expansion of credit under the plan "will not be inflationary if the funds made available flow into investment that raises national productivity."[2]

The full-scale program for introducing social capitalism would involve the creation of three tiers of GSOPs—national, state, and local or municipal. SuperStock would become the national tier. States and localities would be authorized, but not required, to establish GSOPs if they so desired. As the attractiveness of GSOPs as a means of financing the transition to a new and more equitable economic order became more and more apparent, there is little doubt that an increasing number of states and localities would do so.

Equally voluntary would be the participation of companies but with the powerful incentive of relief from federal corporate income tax and access to capital for expansion. The federal government would provide the same facility of guaranteeing loans with which to acquire GSOP equity in the state and local as in the national or SuperStock plan.

Most crucial in the transition from the current economy to the brave new world of universal capital ownership would be financing much of this transition through equity rather than debt. As Paul Hawken (1984) observes in *The Next Economy*, and as have many other economists, we are dangerously overloaded with debt—personal, corporate, and government—having been living beyond our means for the past decade or more. Unlike much of the debt created in the last decade, which has been used to finance consumption, the new money created through the financing of GSOP equity purchases would be used to create new productive assets and would be, as Professor Klein notes, noninflationary.

Limitations of space will not permit full exposition of just how the general stock ownership plans would work, and in any event a number of details would become settled only after some actual experience with the plans, which should be introduced gradually in order to provide for feedback based on actual experience.

In spite of these space limitations, two critical aspects of GSOP operation need still to be discussed. One concerns the making of capital investment decisions. At present, these are in the first instance made by the individual entrepreneur or by the management of a company and then by the financial community in the form of investment bankers, commercial bankers, and venture capitalists, all depending upon the nature of the capital investment and how it is to be financed through varying proportions of equity, debt, and retained earnings. For publicly traded corporations, each major capital spending plan presented to the national GSOP or SuperStock plan will be reviewed by a committee composed of the same kinds of representatives of the financial community now involved in external review of capital spending decisions by corporate management. Also involved will be representatives of consumer, environmental, public health, union, and other groups that have a stake in such investment decisions.[3] Bad judgments will still be penalized by a fall in stock market prices (GSOPs will never, as a matter of policy, acquire more than 49 percent of the equity in any enterprise), but the overall value of the GSOP equity fund will be cushioned against such adverse circumstances by very wide distribution of risk.

In the case of state and local GSOPs, which will channel citizen investment primarily into privately held companies, GSOP investment committees will need to be created to perform a similar review function. These will be composed, as in the case of the national GSOP, of representatives from the financial community and include other stakeholders in the enterprise such as consumers and employees.

Equally critical is how GSOPs would deal with business failures, as there surely will be some. The first point has already been made—namely, the impact would be greatly cushioned by spreading the risk very widely. Second, when companies joined GSOP, they would have to agree to give GSOP equity first claim on company assets in the event of bankruptcy—and the personal assets of the owner or top managers (at least up to some given percentage) in order to prevent unscrupulous owners or managers from milking a company of its assets and then letting it slide deliberately into bankruptcy. Beyond that, companies participating in GSOPs would be obliged to submit quarterly reports to their citizen owners through the GSOP just as they do to their present stockholders, and these would be monitored in order to flag companies getting into trouble. When that occurred, special "troubled company rescue teams" would be constituted to see if a way could not be found to get the company back on a positive course, or, if not, to explore merger with another enterprise so that to the extent possible the jobs invovled would be maintained—or if they could not, that the workers would be retrained for and absorbed into alternative occupations. It is important to emphasize that GSOPs would not provide a vehicle for highly risky new business start-ups. That vital dimension of the U.S. economy would very likely, however, be greatly invigorated as the investment banking community, no longer so signficantly involved in financing capital investment decisions of established companies, began to turn its attention more and more to the venture capital arena.

NOTES

[1]Defined here as a set of economic and political arrangements that will lead to a more equitable and widespread distribution of ownership of productive assets, resulting ultimately in greater self-governance through user ownership of housing and community facilities and more democratic local private ownership and control of the means of pro-

ducing goods and services and the credit required to finance such production. This definition is based on Turnbull (1975).

[2] A formal report on the Brookings Institution Seminar on Policies for Capital Diffusion through Expanded Equity Ownership was never issued, but informal notes are available from the author at the Council on International and Public Affairs, 777 United Nations Plaza, New York, New York 10017.

[3] E.F. Schumacher developed some interesting ideas on representation of broader community interests through what he calls social councils to determine how corporate revenues in the public domain should be used in the next to the last chapter in *Small Is Beautiful* (1973). Also relevant is Shann Turnbull's pioneering work on stakeholders; see various of his contributions to Morehouse (1983).

REFERENCES

Hawken, Paul. *The Next Economy*. New York: Ballantine Books, 1984.

Morehouse, Ward (ed.). *The Handbook of Tools for Community Change*. New York: Intermediate Technology Group of America, 1983.

Schumacher, E.F. *Small Is Beautiful*. New York: Harper and Row, 1973.

Turnbull, Shann. *Democratizing the Wealth of Nations*. Sydney: Company Directors Association of Australia, 1975.

SuperStock: a conservative alternative
to the welfare state

Robert Lekachman

The author is Distinguished Professor of Economics at Herbert H. Lehman College, City University of New York.

The notion of SuperStock is ingenious. The Speiser SuperStock proposal is feasible and it is very carefully worked out. From a political standpoint, it goes very much with the grain of American faith in market capitalism. It is an extension of the idea of property ownership.

We are a highly conservative, capitalist society. In fact, if I were engaged in marketing the SuperStock concept, I would present it as a basically conservative notion. If the Reagan Administration is open to any new ideas in its second term, there would be a distinct possibility that the Administration would perceive this idea as consistent with the ethos of ownership which runs through the official family.

The question that I wish briefly to examine is, if we accept SuperStock as feasible, as indeed I do, will it fulfill the promise of humanizing capitalism by spreading the benefits of ownership universally and diminish the unnecessary inequality of income and wealth in our society?

SuperStock, as a notion, appears to have some fairly severe limitations. First, it would leave our system of capitalism basically unchanged. SuperStock will not change workplace relationships, it will not improve worker participation. British Socialists were, somewhat naively, shocked right after the Second World War when, in the wake of nationalization of railroads, coal mines, and other industries, they discovered that workers still struck against nationalized boards, just as they struck against private operators. Running the flag of the British Coal Authority over a mine pit, and doing little else, left utterly unchanged hierarchical relationships within the workplace. Nationalization alone left essentially unchanged the essential alienation of workers from their product and their work; in fact, it left in place one of the more destructive aspects of capitalism.

This is even more true for the SuperStock scheme because the ownership rights contemplated are deprived of many of the traditional attributes of stock ownership in a capitalist economy. Workers will not be able to vote the stock; therefore they will have no control of the policies of the 2,000 large corporations whose stocks are involved. Workers will not be able, except possibly via inheritance, to dispose of the stock.

In fact, this SuperStock proposal is ultimately not terribly different, in principle, from a notion that helped George McGovern lose the 1972 Presidential election: the Demo-grant, which was a universal $1,000 per person distribution to the entire population. The Demo-grant was derided as welfare.

I must be careful, however, to differentiate the Demo-grant from SuperStock. The latter grant is to be financed on sound principles out of future profits. Nevertheless it still is, in effect, a grant unrelated to the individual merit of the recipient. It is still subject, I suggest, to attack on essentially anti-McGovern grounds.

SuperStock is, however, a better notion than the employee stock ownership plans (ESOP) because each of the ESOPs is subject to the difficulty that, if the company goes broke, the workers will find themselves with a defunct property. Their faith is tied to the prosperity of an individual enterprise. There is a good insurance principle operating in StuperStock, on the other hand, since ownership rights are spread over 2,000 large corporations rather than one; if one or a handfull fail, the remainder will presumably pick up the slack.

I personally find distressing the substitution of SuperStock distributions for our rather flimsy structure of social welfare. The very term welfare, of course, in our society, has become invidious—a very sad development indeed. Properly conceived and administered as in the Scandinavian nations and in Western Europe more generally, however, welfare programs create the very bonds of common citizenship that Speiser is striving for through universal stock ownership. What has cushioned the impact of an unemployment rate in Western Europe even more serious than the rate in the United States in 1981-82 has been a more fully developed—I must use the word—welfare state.

With SuperStock, we should, it seems to me, be moving away from the creation of common interest in protecting the unemployed, the elderly, the victims of medical misfortune, the handicapped, and other vulnerable groups. We ought to be moving in the direction of decent provision for all of these groups, as rights rather than charity. I fear that SuperStock represents, from this perspective, a retreat from movement towards a more humane society. From my point of view, instead of advocating a movement away from Social Security and related benefits, I unrepentantly advocate a movement toward a more decent provision of such benefits—a movement toward some sort of Swedish model of social arrangements.

The above constitute serious reservations about the concept of SuperStock, but if we assume that Ronald Reagan is not an isolated phenomenon, that in fact he does represent an accentuation of the very strong vein of American conservatism, of American preference for business activity over public activity, then SuperStock is an excellent alternative to the welfare state.

SuperStock is genuinely a conservative notion. In an era that threatens to be conservative for some time to come, it's going to be ideas that are either conservative or at least can be presented as conservative that are going to stand some chance in the political marketplace. If President Reagan is to be followed by a younger conservative then SuperStock ought to have a constituency—a natural constituency—among conservatives. Within the conservative context it is indeed a distinct improvement over current arrangements, even though people of my disposition would vastly prefer a dramatically different capitalist reorganization.

APPENDIX C

HOW AND WHY PEOPLE BUILD CAPITAL

by George Copeman and Carol Arrowsmith

When a business is successful beyond a modest level, it can build capital at a very fast rate. A steady but high rate of profitability creates a geometric rate of capital growth, much of it achieved with tax relief. The self-financing aspect of successful business is important for national prosperity, but it is divisive if the capital created is not shared with employees. No amount of cash profit sharing can make up for employees missing out on the capital growth. Moreover, any attempt to make up by generous cash profit sharing for not sharing the capital growth, actually stunts the growth by distributing money which should have been reinvested in the business.

So we see here a conflict of interest which can only be reconciled by employee shareholding, aided by tax reliefs parallel to those available for the successful business. The question is, which types of employee share schemes are most suited to a particular company's need? There are three main types of scheme favoured with tax relief in Britain.

A CHOICE OF SHARE SCHEMES

Profit Sharing

A profit sharing share scheme operates on the basis of an annual allocation of a portion of the company's pre-tax profits, to be used by trustees to acquire shares which are then appropriated to eligible employees. The amount of profit used can be governed by a formula relating it to the performance of the company or it may be entirely at the discretion of the board of directors but, in either case, it will generally be subject to the guideline limits recommended by investment protection committees (non-statutory bodies representing the major institutional investors). The trustees may use the money either to purchase shares from existing shareholders or to subscribe new issue shares at market price, or both. The money so applied is allowable for corporation tax relief.

The shares acquired must be appropriated to eligible employees on similar terms; this generally means that the allocation may be either the same for all employees, or in proportion to earnings, or weighted in favour of those having longer service, or by some other acceptable criteria or combination thereof. Differences explicitly based on status or on board discretion are not permitted. All full-time employees (usually those contracted to work at least 25 hours per week) with five years' service or more must be eligible to participate; inclusion of part-timers and the setting of a shorter period of service for qualification are at the discretion of the company.

Shares, once appropriated, are the beneficial property of the participant and cannot be taken away except in bankruptcy proceedings against the individual. The participant must, however, contract to leave the shares in the hands of the trustees for at least two years, except in circumstances of death, retirement, redundancy or leaving work by reason of injury or incapacity, and for five years if they are to be received completely free of income tax.

Savings-related

A participant in a savings-related share option scheme must enter into a SAYE (Save-As-You-Earn) contract with a building society or the Department of National Savings, agreeing to save a regular sum (currently between £10 and £100 a month) for five years. At the end of this period he receives a bonus equal to (currently) fourteen monthly payments and, if he leaves the savings in the account for a further two years, a second bonus of the same amount, both bonuses being tax-free. Upon entering into the SAYE contract he is granted an option to subscribe for ordinary shares of the company. The price per share is fixed at the discretion of the board, subject to a lower limit of 10 percent less than the current market price. The aggregate option price is usually equal to the sum which the participant will have saved plus the bonuses after five years or after seven years—the period depending on his own decision at the outset.

For an employee leaving the company before completing at least three years of his SAYE contract, the option lapses. There are compassionate exceptions under which the option can be exercised early, but only to the extent of the money which has actually been accumulated in the SAYE account up to that time. All full-time employees with five years service must be eligible to participate in the scheme.

Discretionary options

Participation in an executive share option scheme is entirely at the discretion of the board of the company, both as to participants and to the extent of their participation (though mindful of the guideline limits recommended by investment protection committees). The options granted to executives, if they are to qualify for tax relief, are exercisable not less than three years after the date of grant (to avoid suspicion that participants are taking advantage of inside information) but not more than ten years after the date of grant. So there is a seven-year "window" when they can be exercised. Options cannot be granted below the market price of the shares nor exercised at intervals of less than three years, if there is to be tax relief. An option can, however, be exercised after the employee has left the company, if the scheme rules allow this, or within one year of the employee's death (even if the option has not been held for three years). Both these cases, however, are subject to the ten-year limit on the life of the option. Because options cannot generally be exercised during the first three years after grant, the scheme can provide that for some or all of this period the option lapses if the employee leaves to take another job elsewhere.

There is no income tax on the difference between the market price of the shares when the option is granted and the market price when the shares are sold, if the latter is higher. These gains are, however, chargeable to capital gains tax when the shares are sold, if they exceed the taxpayer's annual limit of tax-free gains.

A CHOICE OF SAVINGS MEDIA

There are four main ways in which most people accumulate personal capital in Britain with tax relief: firstly, by buying a house, having borrowed money to do so, and receiving tax relief on the interest paid on the mortgage loan; secondly, by belonging to an occupational pension scheme. All the contributions to it, by the employer and the employee, are free of tax and so are the dividends and interest on the investments purchased by the pension fund. When you retire, the amount of capital built up by the fund for you is used to pay you (and usually also any dependant) a monthly income until death.

The third method is by belonging to an employee share scheme. This is more recent and on a smaller scale, so far. (There are at the time of writing only 1610 approved employee share schemes but they have grown in number by 80 per cent in the last six months.) However, calculations made by the authors together with Professor Peter Moore, principal of the London Business School, and published in their book *Shared Ownership* show that if an employee belongs to a share scheme throughout the whole of his or her working life and the employing company is moderately successful, in terms of profitability, throughout the whole of this period, the amount of capital built up could be as great as the value of the employee's house. Of course there is the risk that the firm may not be continuously successful. On the other hand, employees may by good work and good fortune make it very successful and build even more capital.

The fourth way of building up capital, with tax relief, is to set up your own business and if it is successful, spend some of its profits on making it grow.

All economic life is risky and it is generally a good idea to be building some capital through home ownership, some through belonging to a pension scheme and some through belonging to one or more employee share schemes—or alternatively setting up your own business and of course allowing your employees to share in your good fortune, if you succeed.

Those who do not work for an organisation which can provide them with the opportunity of share ownership—such as the public service—usually have better pensions.

APPENDIX D

Excerpt from *City Periscope*, The Journal of the City SDP,Summer/Autumn 1985, p. 6

Wider Share Ownership

Regular readers of the *City Periscope* may note some pleasing similiarities between the proposals in the new Open Forum pamphlet: "Equality and Opportunity in an Enterprise Economy" and the draft proposals of our own policy study group, "Winning Together," which were published in our spring issue. Undoubtedly this is due in part to the presence of Roger Carroll, the convenor of our own policy study group, on the national SDP's working party on share ownership, which was chaired by Jeremy Hardie. The Open Forum discussion paper No 11 is available from the SDP, Cowley Street, London SW1P 3NB, price £1 plus 20p p&p.

The main proposals are:

Profit sharing

We want to give a boost to employee profit-sharing, which is the most straightforward, and so probably the best way of achieving a quick and widespread change in how employees participate in the success or failure of their company. We therefore recommend that:

(a) Pay received as bonus is taxed at a concessionary rate—say 20%—instead of 30%

(b) Companies which pay more than 5% of their wage bill in bonus get 10% off their corporation tax bill.

(c) If an inflation tax were introduced by an Alliance Government, the tax penalties for overshooting the pay norm should be reduced if the excessive increase includes profit-sharing, or eliminated if it is taken in the form of shares.

The cost of these tax concessions should be limited (as are for example the costs of the loan guarantee scheme, for ECGD insurance) so as not to impose an open-ended burden on the Exchequer. The limit must be high enough to give the scheme a chance to make a real impact. We suggest £1/2bn pa.

Employee share ownership

We propose to build on the changes initiated by the Government in 1978 under the Lib/Lab pact to encourage employee share ownership, and on the tax incentives set out in the SDP's policy document on industrial democracy.

Customer share ownership

We intend to hand over a minority (say 30%) of the shares of the monopoly utilities to their customers. These shares would not be saleable but would carry dividends and voting rights. Customers would be able to elect representatives to the Boards. This measure will redistribute income and wealth; widen share ownership; and, most important, give power to consumers. A proportion (say 10%), of the utilities should also be owned by employees.

The justice of ths proposal, as compared with what the Conservatives intend to do with British Gas, is very important. The utilities belong to the public as customers, because it is they who have paid the bills which have paid off the debt and created the equity which is now to be sold to private shareholders. The Conservatives should not sell off this equity until a General Election has confirmed that there is public support for denying customers what we would offer them.

Citizen's share ownership

We also discuss how to increase citizen's share ownership—that is, the number and range of people who own shares in British industry at large, not just in the company for which they work, or in public utilities. This can redistribute wealth, give everyone a stake in the overall prosperity of British industry, and do something for those in the public service who cannot have employee share schemes.

There are three basic options:

(1) To encourage purchase of shares by tax incentives—either of the kind used in France under the Loi Monory; or, more likely, via the radical reforms proposed in the SDP's Green Paper on the reform of taxation, which will encourage personal investment in shares.

(2) To redistribute income and widen share ownership further by creating a citizens' trust in which every adult citizen has a stake. This trust could own 10% of all private sector enterprises over a certain size, shares to be acquired by requiring companies to issue new shares to the trust each year. This could be done either by using a proportion of profits to buy existing shares or, if the enterprise concerned preferred, by scrip issue. After tax deductibility we estimate that cost as equivalent to an increase in corporation tax of about 2 1/2%, but the cash remains in the company.

This trust could build up over 20 years, until it amounts to 10% of the enterprises involved. The trust would also hold most (say 60%) of the shares in the utilities (after customers and employees have had theirs). Together with customer ownership such a trust might provide £100-£150 pa income to each citizen. The citizens trust would administer the collection of shares and distribution of dividends—it would *not* participate in the control of private or public sector industries.

(3) To distribute shares in the public utilities to all citizens as a free gift.

Options for the status of the new shares

All our share ownership proposals raise the question whether the shares which people get as employees, or citizens, or customers, should be saleable straightforwardly as most other shares now are (though not those acquired under such schemes as the Business Expansion Scheme or current Employee Share Ownership schemes). Generally, we do not think they should.

The point of widening share ownership is to make people identify more closely with the fortunes of their company; or of the country; or with the profits and performance of the utilities; and these goals require that people are and remain shareholders.

If they sell their shares at once—as full saleability would allow—the exercise becomes simply a complicated way of handing out near-cash to all and sundry. If that is what is intended, it would be better to target the hand out more specifically, by giving direct cash help to those who need it.

Our proposals are to do with shareholding and its beneficial effects, not simply redistribution; even though redistribution is certainly one of the objectives served—by, for example, the citizens' unit trust scheme; the hand out to customers of utility shares; and the tax incentives for employee and personal share ownership.

Taken together, our proposals can be seen as to a three-tiered plan to transform Britain.

(1) The opportunity for every man and every woman to share, every year or six months, in their company's profits, with tax incentives;

(2) Employee share schemes to enable all company employees to build up a large personal investment in their company's shares over a number of years, with tax incentives;

(3) Broader personal investment in a variety of shares, including privatised public utilities, through tax incentives, or a citizen's unit trust, or free gifts of shares in the public utilities to citizens.

BIBLIOGRAPHY

Albus, James S. *Peoples' Capitalism: The Economics of the Robot Revolution*. Kensington, Maryland: New World Books, 1976. (Note: This book is available in Great Britain from Mr. V.R. Hadkins, Social Credit Centre, 32 Totley Grange Rd., Sheffield S17 4AF, England.)

Azar, Edward E. "Development Diplomacy," *A Shared Destiny* (Joyce R. Starr, ed.). New York: Praeger Publishers, 1983.

Azar, Edward E. "U.S. Comprehensive Regional Policy for the Middle East," *Global Policy Challenge of the 80s* (Morton A. Kaplan, ed.). Washington, D.C.: Washington Institute for Values in Public Policy, 1984.

Blinder, Alan S. "Economic Policy Can be Hard-Headed—and Soft-Hearted," *Business Week*, August 12, 1985.

Brittan, Samuel. "Economic Viewpoint," *Financial Times*, London, July 4, 1985.

Brittan, Samuel. *Jobs, Pay, Unions and the Ownership of Capital*. London: Financial Times, 1984.

Brittan, Samuel. "Thatcherism and Beyond," *Encounter* magazine, April, 1985.

Brittan, Samuel. "The Case for Capital Ownership for All," *Financial Times*. London, September 20, 1984.

Brittan, Samuel. *The Role and Limits of Government: Essays in Political Economy*. London: Temple Smith, 1983.

Butler, Stuart M. *Privatizing Federal Spending: A Strategy to Eliminate the Deficit*. New York: Universe Books, 1985.

Copeman, George. *Employee Share Ownership and Industrial Stability*. London: Institute of Personnel Management, 1975.

Copeman, George. *Leaders of British Industry*. London: Gee Co., 1955.

Copeman, George. *The Challenge of Employee Shareholding*. London: Business Publications, 1958.

Copeman, George. *The Changing Pattern of Savings and Investment in the United Kingdom*. London: Conference of the British-North American Committee, June, 1976.

Copeman, George. *The Chief Executive and Business Growth*. London: Leviathan House, 1971.

Copeman, George; Moore, Peter; Arrowsmith, Carol. *Shared Ownership: How to Use Capital Incentives to Sustain Business Growth*. Aldershot, England: Gower Publishing Company Limited, 1984.

Copeman, George and Rumble, Tony. *Capital as an Incentive*. London: Leviathan House, 1972.

Davenport, Nicholas. *Memoirs of a City Radical*. London: Weidenfeld and Nicolson, 1974.

Davenport, Nicholas. *The Split Society*. London: Victor Gollancz Ltd., 1964.

Davidson, Paul; Lekachman, Robert; Morehouse, Ward; Speiser, Stuart M. "Symposium on Broadening Capital Ownership," *Journal of Post Keynesian Economics*, Volume 7, No. 3. Armonk, New York: M.E. Sharpe, Inc., 1985.

Fay, C.R. *Copartnership in Industry*. Cambridge, England: Cambridge Univ. Press, 1913.

Ferrara, Peter. *Social Security Reform*. Washington, D.C.: Heritage Foundation, 1982.

Galbraith, John Kenneth. *Almost Everyone's Guide to Economics*. New York: Bantam, 1978.

Goodman, John C. "Private Alternatives to Social Security: The Experience of Other Countries," *Cato Journal*, Volume 3, Number 2. Fall 1983.

Goodman, John C. *Social Security in the United Kingdom: Contracting Out of the System*. Washington, D.C.: American Enterprise Institute, 1981.

Hamrin, Robert. *Managing Growth in the 1980s: Toward a New Economics*. New York: Praeger Publishers, 1980.

Heller, Robert. *Shares for Employees*. London: Poland Street Publications Ltd., 1984.

Jay, Peter. *The Crisis for Western Political Economy*. London: Andre Deutsch, 1984.

Job Ownership, Ltd. *Employee Ownership—Why, How?* London: Job Ownership Ltd., 1985.

Joint Economic Committee of Congress. 1976 Joint Economic Report. Washington, D.C.: Joint Economic Committee, 1976.

Kautsky, Karl. "Is Soviet Russia a Socialist State?" *Social Democracy vs. Communism.* New York: The Rand School Press, 1946.

Kelso, Louis O. and Adler, Mortimer J. *The Capitalist Manifesto.* New York: Random House, 1958.

Kelso, Louis O. and Adler, Mortimer J. *The New Capitalists.* New York: Random House, 1961.

Kelso, Louis O. and Hetter, Patricia. *Two-factor Theory: The Economics of Reality.* New York: Vintage Books, 1968.

Keynes, John Maynard. *How to Pay for the War.* London: Macmillan, 1940.

Keynes, John Maynard. *The General Theory of Employment, Interest and Money.* London: Macmillan, 1936. Harbinger paperback, 1964.

Low, Sir Toby, (later Lord Aldington). *Every Man a Capitalist.* London: Conservative Research Centre, 1958.

Maital, Shlomo. *Minds, Markets Money.* New York: Basic Books, 1982.

McClaughry, John (ed.). *Expanded Ownership.* Fond du Lac, Wisconson: Sabre Foundation, 1972.

McClosky, Herbert and Zaller, John. *The American Ethos: Public Attitudes toward Capitalism and Democracy.* Cambridge: Harvard University Press, 1984.

Meade, James E. *Efficiency, Equality, and the Ownership of Property.* London: George Allen Unwin, Ltd., 1964.

Meade, James E. "Full Employment, New Technologies and the Distribution of Income," *Journal of Social Policy,* Volume 13, Part 2. Cambridge: Cambridge University Press, April 1984.

Meade, James E. "Wage-Fixing Revisited," London: The Institute of Economic Affairs Occasional Paper 72, 1985.

Morehouse, Ward (ed.). *The Handbook of Tools for Community Economic Change.* New York: Intermediate Technology Group of North America, 1983.

National Conference of Catholic Bishops. "Catholic Social Teaching and the U.S. Economy," *Origins,* Volume 15, No. 17. Washington, D.C.: National Catholic News Service, October 10, 1985.

Perry, Jr., John H. *The National Dividend.* New York: Ivan Obolensky, Inc., 1964.

Schumacher, E.F. *Small is Beautiful.* New York: Harper Row, 1973.

Speiser, Stuart M. *A Piece of The Action.* New York: Van Nostrand Reinhold Company, 1977.

Speiser, Stuart M. *How to End the Nuclear Nightmare*. New York: North River Press/Dodd Mead, 1984.

Speiser, Stuart M. *SuperStock*. New York: Everest House, 1982.

Turnbull, Shann. *Democratising the Wealth of Nations*. Sydney, Australia: Company Directors Association of Australia Ltd., 1975.

Von Thunen, Johann Heinrich. *The Isolated State*. Abridged and translated from the 2nd German ed. Oxford, England: Pergamon Press, 1966.

Weitzman, Martin L. *The Share Economy—Conquering Stagflation*. Cambridge: Harvard University Press, 1984.

"Wider Share Ownership—Equality and Opportunity in An Enterprise Economy," SDP Open Forum No. 11. London: Social Democratic Party's Working Party on Share Ownership, 1985.